Secrets W[...]

Ian Wilfred

Secrets We Left In Greece
Copyright © 2018 by Ian Wilfred

This is a work of fiction. Names, characters, places and incidents are used fictitiously and any resemblance to persons living or dead, business establishments, events, locations or areas, is entirely coincidental.

No part of this work may be used or reproduced in any manner without written permission of the author, except for brief quotations and segments used for promotion or in reviews.

ISBN: 978-1717016737

Cover Design: Avalon Graphics
Editing: Nancy Callegari
Proofreading: Maureen Vincent-Northam
Formatting: Rebecca Emin
All rights reserved.

*This book is dedicated to the members of my family
I have shared such special times in Greece with:
Ron, Samantha, Maggie, Annette, Neil and Jean*

Acknowledgements

There are a few people I'd like to thank for getting *Secrets We Left In Greece* out into the world.

The fabulous Rebecca Emin at Gingersnap Books for organising everything for me and who also produced both kindle and paperback books. Nancy Callegari for all the time and effort she spent editing the book, Maureen Vincent-Northam for proofreading, and the very talented Cathy Helms at Avalon Graphics for producing the terrific cover.

Finally for my late mum who is always with me in everything I do.

Chapter 1

It was three o'clock in the morning and Miriam was sitting drinking a cup of tea. She had lost count of how many nights she had been doing this. It must be the third or even the fourth week, and it was getting her down. Throughout her life sleep had never been a problem. Even when she worried about something during the day, the minute her head hit the pillow she'd be asleep and even with the grief and upset she had suffered with the death of her beloved husband, Rex, she had been able to sleep well each night.

The doctor had prescribed sleeping tablets but there was no way that Miriam would take them. The last thing she wanted to do was become dependent on drugs, and as for all the other advice she been given – reading, listening to music, special teas, long walks – the list was endless, nothing seemed to be working.

"Hi, Amy, darling. It's just a quick call. I was wondering whether you've spoken to Nan in the last few days and if she sounded okay as I think that something's not quite right."

"Yes, Mum, I was going to call about the same thing. She's not herself. When we were chatting she did seem a little distant, but when I asked her she just said that she was tired. To be honest, we forget she's seventy. Can I call you back later, as I've got a few calls to make?"

"Okay, darling. By the way, how's Paul?"

"Oh, he's fine. Working as hard as ever, but being self-employed it's twenty-four-seven. Love you lots. Bye for now."

It was a lovely crisp, dry, spring morning and Miriam was going to meet a few friends for lunch. This was something she did every Tuesday, but today she wasn't really in the mood due to being tired and unable to sleep. Today she couldn't pretend and put on an act for her friends as they would be able to see right through it and know there was a problem. She should talk to her daughter, Heather, and granddaughter, Amy, about it but they would only fuss and worry which was the last thing Miriam needed.

The talk over lunch was all about grandchildren and holidays. Each of the four friends had been widowed, and as they had known each other for more than 30 years, Miriam was unable to hide her problem from them.

"Oh, girls, I'm exhausted. I'm still not sleeping the night properly. I have no problems dozing off during the day, although I purposely try and avoid doing that, but the nights just seem to go on for ever."

"Miriam, last week you said that you weren't worried about anything. Are you sure there aren't any problems with Heather or Amy? Anyway, I do think you're right not to take sleeping tablets as they can make you become a bit strange."

"Well, I've Googled your problem, Miriam."

They all laughed, because since Alice had got an iPad from her son, anyone would think she was a computer expert. Google had given her a new lease of life.

"So, Alice. What does the iPad have to say?"

"You may well all laugh at me, but there's so much information on insomnia. It says you need to get to the source of the problem first. It may not necessarily be something that's happening now, but it could be something that happened years and years ago which you've pushed out of your mind and then suddenly it's back and needs sorting out."

They all laughed about that and moved on to planning some summer day trips. Miriam thought she was probably overthinking the problem and it was just part and parcel of getting older. After the lunch she walked the mile home to her flat, although whether there was any truth in what Alice had said did cross her mind.

That night was no different to any other. Miriam went to bed about eleven o'clock and went straight to sleep. However, by one-thirty she was wide awake and from experience she knew the best thing to do was to get up. Otherwise she would make things worse by just lying there tossing and turning. She made herself a cup of tea and walked to the bookshelf.

Miriam loved her books and she was certain there was one she hadn't yet read. She chose a Catherine Cookson novel and settled down on the sofa with her tea to read. As she opened the book, something familiar fell out of it. It was a piece of folded up paper resembling a book mark. Unfolding it, Miriam realised that it was a timetable for the boats going from Holkamos harbour to Paxos. She smiled to herself. The word 'Holkamos' meant only one thing. Happy times! More than that, it meant special times! Miriam began to read her book, yet two hours later she couldn't remember a thing about it as her mind was elsewhere.

The following day Miriam was determined not to be beaten by her sleep problem. She was going to keep herself occupied. The first thing on her list was to declutter her bookshelf. She would go through all her books and take all the ones she'd already finished to the charity shop. As the morning continued she gradually felt better. She had lunch and then cleared out a drawer. Perhaps the answer to her sleep problem was just to declutter!

Amongst all the rubbish in the drawer, tucked right at the bottom, were four old calendars. Miriam sat at the dining table and looked at them. They were dated from 2001 through to 2005. As she flicked through them, it wasn't the everyday appointments, the dentists and hair appointments, which captured her attention, but the photos at the top of each month's page. Stunning views of Holkamos which made her feel both happy and sad at the same time. There were almost 20 years of memories in those photos, each one was a happy one, and Miriam was so pleased to have those memories.

Heather had spent the day in her office – or to be more accurate, her back bedroom. She loved working from home although her job as a book keeper for several businesses was rather mundane. It paid the mortgage though, and as long as she was on top of things it gave her ample time to devote to her real passion – jewellery making and going to craft fairs selling her beautiful wares. Heather's life was good and she realised that. Today, however, was different. For the first time since her father had died nearly ten years previously, she was worried about her mother. Things weren't right and she knew she needed to get to the bottom of it.

"Hi, Mum. How are you? What have you been up to today? Anything nice?"

"Hi, Heather. I'm okay thanks. I've been decluttering, sorting books for the charity shop and going through drawers."

"Did you find anything interesting?"

"Not really. Just some old paperwork. Nothing of any importance or value."

Why didn't she mention the calendars? Come to that, why don't they ever discuss Holkamos? Twenty years of such happy family times spending the six-week school summer holidays there and even her beloved granddaughter didn't ever mention it. Was it because they'd never been back since Rex died or were there other reasons?

"Mum, if something was worrying you, you would tell me?"

"There's nothing wrong, Heather. I'm just a bit tired.

I'm getting old. I can't do as much as I used to."

After the phone call, Heather still didn't feel any better. Something was up and between Amy and herself, they had to find out exactly what the problem was.

That night when Miriam went to bed she took a small biscuit tin that had been in the back of one of the drawers, unopened for years. She realised that this might not be a good idea at such a late time of night, but as she couldn't sleep anyway, she figured that it wouldn't matter much. There were at least 20 Polaroid photos in the box, all black and white, and all taken in Holkamos during that special year. It was strange that neither she nor Rex had ever put them into a photograph album alongside all the other family photos.

This was the reason Miriam wasn't sleeping properly – the summer of 1993 – the year which could have changed everyone's lives forever.

Chapter 2

Miriam slowly opened her eyes and glanced at her bedside clock. Was she dreaming? It was 9.15am. Something must be wrong, she thought, as the last time she looked at the clock it was around midnight. It was also taking her some time to come round as she felt as if she'd been in a really deep sleep. As she lay there half awake, her mind returned to the tin of Polaroid photos. Could her insomnia be related to the summer of 1993? If so, what should she do about it?

Heather couldn't concentrate on her jewellery making – something she had never had a problem with until now. She couldn't stop thinking about her mother, the woman who worried about everyone else. If anyone had a problem they'd go to Miriam as she would always have a solution. Heather remembered that it was 27 years ago when she had gone to her mum with a life-changing issue and what had Miriam said? "It's happened. Let's just get on with it. No one's died and life will go on," and so it had. The phone ringing brought Heather back from her thoughts.

"Hi, Mum, it's only me. I was thinking whether we should arrange to go to Nan's on Saturday, just the two of us and try to find out what's wrong. I know she doesn't like to worry us with things, but I just get the feeling that there's something which isn't quite right."

"That's exactly how I feel, Amy. I'll call her and let her know. Shall we say around lunch time?"

"Yes, that's fine, Mum. You don't think she's ill and isn't telling us?"

"All I know is that things aren't right, and the quicker she tells us the sooner we can help to resolve it."

*

After such a slow start to the day, Miriam decided to take it easy. She checked on her neighbour Clive's cat in the flat below hers. This was a routine she carried out every day while he was out at work. It was the only constant thing in her life. Everything else happened when or if she wanted to do it but feeding Cheesy the cat was a must. As she descended the stairs to the flat below she could hear the cat meowing. It wasn't as if he was hungry. He just wanted a little bit of company. Her days of playing with him were over as he wasn't interested in toys anymore. He just liked a stroke and a bit of attention. As she was leaving, she left a little note for Clive and heard that upstairs her phone was ringing.

"Oh, hello, Mum. You sound out of breath."

"No, I've just been down to check on Cheesy."

"That's such a funny name for a cat."

"Yes, I know, darling, but when he was a kitten he was so excited by the smell of cheese, that's how he got his name."

"It's just a quick call to say that I've no craft fairs on this Saturday, so Amy and I thought we'd pop over for a bit of lunch, if that's okay with you."

"That would be lovely as actually I've something to tell you – or should I say ask both of you."

There – she had said it now and there was no backing out of it. This was really most unlike her. Normally she would take days or even months to think things through, but this had come to her in a flash. Was it the right thing to do?

It was now lunch time, so Miriam made a sandwich and poured herself a glass of wine; something she would never dream of doing at midday, but she felt that the afternoon ahead needed a glass or two. After lunch she opened the blanket box in her bedroom, an act she hadn't done since the day she had moved in, filling it with all her photo albums. Where should she start?

There were so many. When Rex was alive he spent hours looking at the photographs, calling her in from the kitchen every five minutes and asking her whether she could remember when a certain one was taken. All of them were happy times!

Miriam was interrupted by a knock at the door, and as she went to answer it she glanced at the clock and saw that it was already 6.30 pm. She had been sitting there going through all the photograph albums for five hours. Where had the time gone?

'Hi, Miriam. I got your note. How can I help?"

"Well, Clive, I was wondering if you could spare me an hour at any time during the week to do something for me on your computer."

"Of course. Give me half an hour to get sorted and I'll come back up."

"Are you sure tonight's alright?"

"Of course it is. See you later."

Miriam still wasn't entirely sure that this was the right thing to be doing, but she poured another glass of wine, put all the photo albums away and moved the coffee table nearer the sofa. No, she was doing the right thing. Clive then returned and plugged in his computer.

"So, Miriam, hit me with it. What do you want me to do?"

"I want to book a holiday for myself, my daughter and my granddaughter. It's a surprise for them."

"Oh, that's a lovely idea. Where are you thinking of going?"

"One of the Greek islands. It's called Holkamos."

"I've never heard of it, Miriam."

"Not a lot of people have, but once you've been there you don't tell anyone about it as you don't want it to get busy and spoilt. The part we stayed on was called Volmos and we spent the six-week school summer holidays there every year for seventeen years."

"Please tell me all about it."

"Oh, we first went when Amy was a baby, but we've not been back since Rex died. It's such a magical place. You fly to Preveza on the Greek mainland and Holkamos is about an hour's ferry ride away. When we first started going, you'd get off the plane and your cases would be on a trolley on the runway and then you'd go through a little wooden hut to show your passport. Things have changed now. It's a proper airport. To get from Preveza to Holkamos, you're taken by coach to the docks and that's where the magic starts, standing on deck, the sun shining and a little cool breeze, and then it's there right in front of you. I always say its calling out, "Come and visit me." Oh yes, Clive, it's a magical place."

"It sounds just like Paradise."

"Oh, it is, but arriving there is just the beginning. Once you've left the ferry and got back onto the coach it's about half an hour to Holkamos Town. The journey there is beautiful with the sea on your left and the mountains on the right. Looking out to sea on a clear day you can spot other islands and then you arrive in the small harbour town with its little cafes and bars. There's nothing big and brash, just quaint. Yes, Clive, to me it is Paradise."

"Are you okay, Miriam? Is something the matter?"

"No, I don't think so. It's just that I've not talked about Holkamos for years, and to be really honest I've not thought about it either. It's a very special place and I think I've realised that perhaps I've missed it far more than I thought."

"Now this looks like a nice place. Two double bedrooms and it says that it's only a five-minute walk to the beach. Guess what? It's on Volmos."

"No. Oh no, Clive. I want us to stay in Holkamos town this time, the completely opposite end. We probably won't go over to Volmos. We'll just stay on the town beach."

Clive was a little surprised about this, but Miriam obviously had her reasons. They spent the next hour or so going through all the options and finally settled on a new build set slightly back from the quayside. It had two bedrooms, a kitchen / lounge and a little balcony where you could stand out and see the sea. Miriam was overjoyed. Clive booked it and said that he'd print everything off when he went back to his flat

Miriam's heart was still racing an hour later. Had she done the right thing? What would Amy and Heather have to say? What if they refused to go? Could she go all that way by herself? The one thing she was sure about was that she had to go. There were things that needed to be put to rest and now was the time to do it.

Chapter 3

It was now May; the start of the holiday season, and the first planes had started to arrive in Preveza. The residents and businesses on Holkamos had spent most of April getting ready for the influx of holiday makers. The next five months would be hectic and everyone had to work hard and earn enough money to see themselves through the winter.

Carolina had spent all her life balancing her work and family commitments while trying to earn a living, but this year it was all about her two grandchildren. She was looking forward to caring for them while her son, Andréas, and her daughter-in-law, Katia, were working. Having a five and seven-year-old every day was more of a pleasure than a handful, and something Carolina was so excited about. Would she be saying the same come the end of September?

Katia didn't work as many hours as Andréas and her job was only a couple of minutes' walk from the family home in the little village of Creakos. Andréas was returning to his job as a waiter down in Holkamos harbour, and despite it being a seven day a week position and more than 150 days until he would have a day off, he was glad to go back. The winter had been difficult, working with the olive trees and labouring jobs and so he was happy to be going back to serving the holiday makers, having a laugh with the other waiting staff and just like every summer, he was pleased that the warm Greek sunshine was on its way.

Up on the hill leading to the castle, Edelina had spent the last couple of weeks preparing her little shop for the holiday season. New stock had arrived from Athens and this was the time which she loved the most, although she always felt nervous. Had she chosen the right stock? Fashion was always such a fickle industry. One minute everyone wanted a certain top and the next it's out of fashion, but with the remainder of the previous year's stock, she was confident that all would be well. She sat drinking her coffee on her little balcony, so pleased to be back in Holkamos. She had only been in Germany for two months visiting her family, but this was her home now and the 12 years she had been here were very special.

Down on Volmos it was a busy few days for Melvin. The holiday home was ready, it had needed a lick of paint to freshen up the bedrooms and now he was all set for his first visitors of the season. He still couldn't believe he was doing this all by himself and not having his lovely Pearl beside him, even though she used to push him along and tell him to get out of the way.

It was now Saturday and Miriam had managed to have a calmer few days. Her good news was that she was now back to having a good night's sleep. A few days ago she had been slightly worried about Heather and Amy's reaction, but it was too late to think about that now. The holiday was booked. Once the initial shock was over and the excuses as to why they couldn't go were offered, Miriam was sure that everything would be alright.

"Hello, you two. I've made us a cottage pie for lunch. I hope that's okay."

"Perfect, Nan, but what's for pudding?"

"Now, Amy, what do you think there is for pudding?"

"Nan's apple and cinnamon tart with thick custard."

"Yes, you're correct, and it will all be ready in about an hour. I'll go and make us all a coffee."

They sat in the lounge chatting about many things. Heather thought to herself that all the worrying about her mother might have been unnecessary as she was back to being her normal self. Perhaps she was just having a few off weeks. It was such a relief. Lunch was lovely and they finished every scrap. They were certainly a family who liked and appreciated good food.

"That was lovely, Nan. I'll go and make us a cup of tea. You've done enough."

"No, Amy. Let's have a glass of wine instead. It's the weekend and I really fancy some."

No, everything isn't alright, Heather thought. This is so out of character. She's going to tell us something. It can't be a celebration. It must be bad news.

"Wine during the day, Nan. That's unusual for you."

As Amy poured the wine, Heather could tell that Miriam was becoming increasingly anxious and knew she had to help her out. This was her mum. She ought to be able to talk about anything.

"Come on, Mum. What's on your mind? You've not been yourself for a few weeks. You always told me that if no one's died, everything else can be sorted."

"I have got something to tell you all, but I would ask you to please let me finish before you have your say."

They looked at each other and nodded. Both Amy and Heather were thinking the worst; it must be a health issue.

"It's like this. I've booked us all a holiday."

"Oh, Mum, how lovely! But why have you got yourself all worked up? It's such a lovely thing to do."

"Sorry, Heather, but I've not finished. The holiday I've booked for us is to Holkamos and we're going on the first day of the school holidays. It will be for two weeks, rather than the normal six weeks and I've got us a two-bedroomed apartment with a nice balcony which looks out over the harbour."

Miriam could see the colour drain from both their faces. It would be difficult for them as they all had so many memories of being there with Rex, but the real reason Miriam needed to return to Holkamos was something she could never tell them. It was for her to sort out. They both started to talk at the same time.

"Mum, I'm so sorry, but I'm far too busy. You and Amy can go. That would be really nice. I really am sorry, Mum."

"No, Nan. You and Mum go. Both Paul and I have far too much on. I can't leave the business as it's just beginning to take off. I'm sorry, Nan."

"You both work from home on a computer. The apartment we'll be staying in has Internet connection, so I think that's the problem solved. I'll pour us another glass of wine and we can toast our two weeks in the beautiful Greek sunshine."

Nothing more was said, although not a lot of talking was had about anything more than Clive's cat and Miriam's lunches with her friends. It was all just general chit chat, and then at about four o'clock Amy and Heather left.

"Hi, Paul, I'm home."

"I'm in the office. How was your lunch? More importantly, how's your Nan?"

Amy explained all about the holiday and that there was no way that she could take time away from work. She did social media for companies which had paid for a seven-day service. Holidays didn't come into the equation.

"Amy, what was the problem with Miriam that you and your Mum were both worried about? This is the perfect situation to make sure she's alright. All your work is done on the iPad, which makes everything so easy. Go and have fun with the two most important people in your life. Anyway, you've not said where the holiday is."

"No, I'm not going. I'm not in the mood for a holiday and certainly not one in Holkamos. Would you like a drink? I'm going to have a gin and tonic."

Paul left her alone for an hour and carried on with what he was doing. However, he knew he had to say something. He was sure that Amy's reaction would be different if it was anywhere else in the world. What was it with Holkamos?

Heather closed her front door and screamed, "Why have you done it, Mum? Of all the places in the world, Holkamos is bottom of my list, and as far as I'm concerned doesn't exist anymore. How can I get out of it without hurting her? She was right. I could work from there if I needed to. My clients have holidays and of course they'll understand if I take two weeks off. As for the craft fairs, July and August are the quietest months, so I have no excuse not to go apart from not wanting to. Why don't I want to? I'm scared.

"Amy, I can tell this has really upset you and it's a decision you have to make, but if I could just say one thing, I promise I won't mention it again. All the years we've been together it's a subject you shy away from. Also, when I've been with your Mum and Nan, they don't like talking about it either. At first, I thought it was because Rex had died and all the memories it brought back, but it can't be as you all talk about Christmases together and weekends away. Rex is discussed all the time without such upset or sadness. Just happy times you all spent together, but for some reason the three of you will not talk about Holkamos after nearly twenty years of happy holidays. I really don't understand. This might sound stupid, but did something really bad happen? Did someone die? Worse than that, was anyone murdered?"

"Don't be so silly, Paul. They were very happy times. No one died and I have lots of happy memories of my holidays there. I just don't want to go back. I've moved on from that."

"What's the 'that', Amy? Why do you need to move on from something that brings back happy memories? What happened that was so bad?"

"Nothing happened. Just stop questioning me. I'm not a criminal."

"Okay, I won't mention it again and it's for you to sort out with your mum and nan, but this is my final word on the subject. All the time we've been discussing this, you've fiddled with that ring on your finger, the ring that you've worn since the day we met, the ring you never take off, the ring that obviously means so much to you. Something happened in Holkamos all those years ago and perhaps now is the time to get it sorted."

Chapter 4

It had been nearly a week since Miriam had heard from either Amy or Heather, but it didn't worry her. The holiday was booked and it was now only a couple of months away. She had wondered whether it might have been better to go by herself, get a little apartment or a hotel room and stay for a month, but the reaction on their faces told her that they to needed to go back to Holkamos for reasons she didn't understand.

Paul and Amy carried on as if nothing had happened. The only difference was that Amy was very conscious about drawing any attention to her little ring. Perhaps after all these years she should take it off. It belonged to the past, over ten years previous, and it didn't match any of her other jewellery, but it did mean everything to her. Perhaps the time was right to say goodbye to the ring and the place to do that could be Holkamos.

"Hi, Nan. Just a quick call to let you know I've sorted out all my work commitments and I'll be fine for the holiday."

"Oh, I'm so pleased, Amy. Thank you so much. Something tells me it will be a very special holiday."

Heather felt bad about not having spoken to Miriam, but what could she say? She still hadn't come up with a good enough excuse to not go and the one thing she wasn't going to do was lie. Her mum was the most important person in her life. When, at 19, she'd returned home from university, pregnant, her mum's reaction had been supportive. "Okay, we'll deal with it. It's happened to other families in the past and will continue to happen. How exciting! I'm going to be a grandmother. Miriam had taken her and Amy in and brought Amy up so that she could study to become an accountant. Her parents had never asked any questions about Amy's father and Miriam had only loved and cared for her. All she wants to do is take me on holiday, she mused. A holiday I don't want to go on, a holiday I can't go on.

Paul was pleased that Amy had agreed to go on the holiday. He hadn't talked about it again, but when she told him that she would be going, all he said was, "If that's what you really want to do, I'm happy for you. Amy had told her mum she had agreed to go, and Heather was pleased, but it still didn't make things any easier. Her head felt as if it was about to explode. Heather talked to Amy and Miriam about everything apart from the reason she didn't ever want to go back to Holkamos. She was strong and able to cope with her demons, but that might not be the same in Greece.

To make up for initially seeming ungrateful, Amy took Miriam on a shopping expedition for holiday clothes. They had a great time choosing clothes for the daytime and slightly over the top evening wear, shoes, handbags, even different makeup. It had been such a fun day!

"You know, Amy, your mum still hasn't told me if she's coming with us. The tickets have arrived, so what should I do? She knows the date and the time and that Clive's taking us to the airport. What more can I do?"

"Nothing, Nan. She hasn't mentioned it to me since the day I phoned to tell that I was going. Neither of us can do anything more, but somehow I don't think she'll want to let you down. We're still a team, even though Grandad's not with us, but I think he'll be around every corner we turn in Greece. I love you so much, Nan. I'm sorry I was so rude about the holiday. I think I need to go back to Holkamos even if it's the last time. I think it's very important."

"Amy, you've taken the words right out of my mouth. I need to go back too. I have my reasons and when I get there I think they'll become very clear. I love you so much. I could not ask for a better granddaughter in all the world."

It was still a few weeks away from the holiday when the doorbell rang. Miriam answered on the intercom.

"Hello, I've got a parcel for you."

Miriam brought the parcel up to her flat and put it on the table. It was quite big, but very light. She couldn't remember ordering anything, but it was addressed to her. As she unwrapped the package, she saw that it contained three towels separately packed in clear polythene bags. Taking the first one out, she saw it was bright blue with large lettering 'Granddaughter' across the top. The second bag also had a towel inside it, but this one said 'Grandmother'. Miriam's heart was racing and she knew she didn't really need to open the next one as it would say 'Daughter' but she still had to just see the word in letters. She was so happy, she knew Heather wouldn't let her down.

"Thank you for the lovely present, darling. You do know we'll have a good time, a very special time."

"I'm sorry, Mum. Really sorry."

"Nothing more to be said, Heather, apart from "Have you got your outfits sorted?"

Chapter 5

It was another sunny morning on the little island of Holkamos, the town was waking up as the holiday makers made their way to the beaches, and boats in the harbour took them out on day trips. The cafes and restaurants were opening and the town was buzzing on this hot sunny July day. Although it was only ten o'clock in the morning, the temperature was already very high. The holiday season was in full swing.

The shopkeepers on the hill going up to the castle were starting to put their stock outside their shops, there was everything from Greek soaps, leather bags, fabulous summer clothes, china and plenty of lovely gifts to tempt the visitors.

Edelina had been to the bakery and picked up some pastries to last her through her 14-hour day. She wasn't complaining. She loved her life on Holkamos, working seven days a week wasn't a hardship and as for her little shop which she had established over the last 12 years, it was very special. The actual selling space was only three metres by ten metres, but that was all she needed to sell her stunning silk tops in every bright colour you could imagine. The other wall featured everything in white. People loved to wear white while they were out at night as it highlighted their tans. Among the clothes were belts, little clutch bags and costume jewellery. Any female coming in could put together a very glamorous look for going out at night to the little restaurants.

Out at the back of the shop was Edelina's little workshop, although actually it had never been used as one. She used it as a general store room but dreamed of using it in the future to create beautiful sarongs. She had bought the rolls of fabric over ten years ago and they were still wrapped in the paper they were delivered in. There's always another season to do that. Perhaps she should do that in the winter when the shop was closed instead of going back to Germany to see her mum, dad, sisters and her beloved nephews and nieces.

Edelina's favourite part of the building was her one bedroomed apartment above the shop with its little balcony looking down into the harbour. That was the reason she had bought the premises. She knew she could make any selling space look good, but it was the living area that needed to be special.

Andréas was on his scooter coming down from Creakos ready to start another day in his uncle's restaurant. He loved Greece and the little island of Holkamos, but he didn't know anything else. This was his birthplace, where he'd been to school and got married. One year was very much like another. The season started slowly in May with the older visitors and built up to a summer climax with all the families arriving, and then slowed down in September. Once the holiday trade had finished, the restaurant closed and Andréas went to work in the olive fields, mending nets and placing them around the trees ready to harvest the olives. The winter months also gave him more time to spend with his wife and two young children. Andréas felt very contented with his life.

"Only another hour, Amy, and we'll be landing. What can you see out of the window? Is your book any good? Heather, why didn't you bring your Kindle with you? It's so much easier and lighter."

"I really don't know. I agree with you, but I prefer an actual book. I've brought five for some strange reason. I feel it would be doing Holkamos an injustice having modern technology with me. I know that sounds so stupid."

"Oh, Mum, that's like going back in time," said Amy. Next you'll be saying you've got a swimsuit and not a bikini."

"I have only brought swimsuits. I'm far too old for anything else."

"Oh, don't be silly. Nan's brought three bikinis, haven't you?"

"Yes, of course. I don't want to be strapped up on my sun lounger. You never know, I might even take the top part off."

The banter on the plane was just an act. All three of them were feeling nervous, but for different reasons. However, it was too late to turn back. They were nearly at Preveza and that's when the holiday would really start.

An hour later they were enjoying the late afternoon sunshine. Miriam had forgotten just how hot Greece was in July and August. Once through customs and having collected their cases, they were directed on to the coach which would take them to the ferry port and then the short journey to the island of Holkamos. Everything was so familiar. It didn't seem like it was ten years since they had last done this trip. The representative in charge of the transfer was talking and pointing things out, but Miriam couldn't remember a word of what was said. She felt very calm, the butterflies of the last few days had disappeared and she seemed to be in a little bubble of her own. Everyone and everything around her was isolated from her. It was very weird, but in a very good way.

"Nan, come on. We're here at the ferry. You are miles away."

"Oh, sorry, darling. I think I was day dreaming."

They had to get off the coach and on to the ferry. This was it. There was no going back. Following each other and then climbing up the stairs to the top deck, they found seats overlooking the horizon. The whole journey was spent in complete silence. Miriam closed her eyes. The movement of the boat and the smell of the sea all felt so normal to her. She was sure this had been the right thing to do.

Amy had spent the time planning how she could manipulate the holiday for a whole two weeks. Perhaps the apartment had a pool, so they wouldn't need to go to the beach at all. The restaurant nearest to the apartment could become their favourite place to eat. She could surely manage it for two weeks.

As for Heather, her mind wasn't focused on how to get through the holiday. There was no need to worry about that. Whatever's going to happen, will happen. No, Heather was thinking about how 20 or even 30 years ago she should have or could have been honest with herself. Now it was far too late to change anything.

They disembarked from the ferry and got onto the coach for the short ride to Holkamos town and little harbour. When the coach came to its destination, they were the only three getting off. The holiday rep pointed them in the direction of a middle-aged Greek lady who welcomed them and showed them up to their lovely, modern apartment. There was one twin bedroom and one double. Amy and Heather said they would share the twin so Miriam could have the double. They joked that this was in case she wanted to entertain a gentleman over the holiday. They all laughed. A bottle of red wine and three bottles of water were in the kitchen. It was nearly early evening by now and Heather and Amy decided to shop for groceries. They needed coffee, milk, tea and more water.

Once they had gone, Miriam changed her clothes, poured herself a glass of wine and went out onto the little balcony. From here she could see the little chapel of Panagia on a rock just a very short stone's throw from the harbour. As she sat there enjoying the gentle breeze, she started to cry like never before. This would never have happened if she hadn't come here. Miriam was so thankful that she was by herself. What could she do to rid herself of these demons in her head? Something told her there would be more days like this and she needed to prepare herself for the worst.

"We're back, Mum. Sorry it took so long. We stopped off for a drink before going shopping. There's a lovely little restaurant just a few metres down from here and as we've all had a long day, we thought we might pop in there for something to eat tonight rather than walk down into the harbour. Is that alright with you?"

"That would be lovely, darlings. I was only just thinking that an early night might be just what I need."

"Nan, I was saying to Mum that up here is a part of Holkamos that we've never really been to. I don't recognise any of it. You can see the castle over to the right and that's not changed a bit. We'll have to explore tomorrow and get our bearings."

Carolina had taken her grandchildren away for a few days to stay with her sister in Newtonos and as a surprise Andréas was having the evening off from the restaurant. He wanted to have an evening with Katia without the children.

"Hello. What are you doing home so early? It's only half past seven and what's in all those bags?"

I thought that seeing as though Mum and the children aren't here, we could make the most of it and have a quiet night in. I'm going to cook us a lovely meal. I've got some wine and we'll just enjoy some time together."

"Oh, Andréas, I do love you. I'm so lucky to have such a loving caring husband."

"I know you do, so why not pour us a drink? I'll have a quick shower and then get cooking."

"Funny you should mention a shower. I was just thinking of having one myself. Do you mind if I join you?"

After the shower they went to bed and before they knew it time had flown by. Andréas started cooking. It was ten o'clock and beginning to get cooler. Two big bowls of pasta were prepared in no time and sitting under one of the lemon trees, it was the perfect end to the day.

"We're so lucky to have two gorgeous children, Katia, but it's always nice to spend time together just the two of us. I love you very much and I know our relationship started out as a bit of fun... Well, actually a lot of fun, and then all the stress and shame of having to get married, but all that fun turned to love. You know that, don't you?"

"Yes, I do now. It took me some time to realise it, but we're good together. It's not easy with two young children and working all the hours we do, but what we have is very special and I don't want anything more out of life, Andréas. If you're happy, then so am I."

"So, what do you think we should do now we've finished eating? How about some more of that fun we both like?"

Back in Holkamos town, Miriam, Heather, and Amy shared a lovely meal and a large carafe of wine, so by the time they got back to the room they were exhausted. Amy and Miriam went straight to bed but Heather got her book, poured herself another glass of wine, lit a citronella candle and went out on to the balcony. Why didn't she want to come here? It was Paradise. There was nowhere in the world she would sooner be. In all her forty plus years, her happiest times were here. Life could be very cruel and only the fittest survive, but in her case could it be the bravest? That's what she lacked, bravery.

Miriam sat up in bed, her head was spinning and she was tired after such a long day. "So you've done it, old girl," she said to herself. "You've come back to Holkamos, so what now? How can coming back here put any secrets to rest? Just looking at Heather and Amy tells me that this is more than just a holiday for all of us. Perhaps the things that happened all those years ago should be left in the past.

Chapter 6

They were all up at around eight-thirty the following morning with coffee and pastries from the little bakery being the order of the day. The three of them squeezed onto the small balcony from where they could see the little boats heading over to the islands and secluded beaches.

All three sat there in a contented silence. Miriam suggested that Amy and Heather should go off and do something together as she was still tired and wasn't in the mood for a day on the beach. Depending on how she felt, she might walk down into the harbour later. Amy and Heather decided to go and spend the day on the beach and they all agreed to meet back at the apartment at around seven, ready to glam themselves up for the evening.

Down on Volmos, Melvin had a busy day ahead. He had just waved goodbye to a family staying in the rental house and he now needed to prepare it for another family arriving. Thankfully they weren't due to land at Preveza for another ten hours so there was plenty of time – three bedrooms, two bathrooms and one large lounge kitchen diner – six hours maximum. He didn't need a gym when he did this every two weeks. For a while after Pearl had died, Melvin considered selling the house, but he was pleased that he hadn't as it had been his saving grace, keeping him busy meeting people. He wasn't good by himself when he had nothing to do.

Once Heather and Amy had gone off to the beach, Miriam had a shower and got herself ready to take a slow stroll down into the town. As she made her way through the little streets everything was coming back to her. Nothing had changed, no structural work, the streets were all just as she had remembered. Restaurant names and furniture were different, but the size of the restaurants was the same. The little fruit and veg shop that had been there since their very first visit was exactly as she remembered it, but the smell of Holkamos! She had missed that, but she hadn't really been aware exactly how much she missed it.

When she got to the harbour she sat in one of the cafes with a nice cool frappe. Oh, how she loved to watch the world go by. This could have been 20 years ago. Everything was just as it used to be. Miriam's mind went back to all the times she and Rex would sit here on the front with a glass of wine while Amy and Heather went off looking in the little shops. The first few years they would come back with a toy or game, but as Amy got older it was clothes and flip flops. The last few years they were here Heather sat with them while a teenage Amy was off having fun with her holiday friends. Such happy times to look back on. Now come on, Miriam, she thought to herself. Pull yourself together. That was the past and this is the future.

Looking at her watch Miriam noticed that it was now 12.30. What could she do for the rest of the day? It was very hot and there would be no shade on the apartment balcony. "Perhaps I could catch the little sea taxi over to Volmos," she considered. She had planned to avoid going there, but deep down she knew that would never happen. As she approached the little boat she could see it was empty as most people had gone early to enjoy a full day on the beach.

Stepping onto the little water taxi she realised there was no going back. As the boat turned, there was the little church on her left and the cliff with the castle on the right. Miriam could feel the butterflies returning to her stomach. A minute later and she was in front of Volmos beach. Despite the hundreds of sunbeds, it looked so perfect, still and peaceful. Even the children playing on the edge of the water were playing quietly. "Oh, Volmos, you were such a big part of mine and my family's lives. Now I'm back I realise how much I've missed you." The journey took barely five minutes and there she was standing on the little wooden jetty. The sun was now very hot and she needed to get in the shade. "Miriam," she said to herself, "You're here now. What are you going to do?"

Miriam turned left and started walking along the edge of the coast. Taking off her sandals and letting the little waves splash on her legs helped to cool her down. The way she was feeling she could have been the only one on the beach, she was in a world of her own. The butterflies in her stomach had now passed. Seeing so many families enjoying the beautiful Greek summer sunshine, many more happy memories flooded back. She walked over a little wooden bridge and onto the little beach where instead of sun loungers, a few people were sunbathing on towels and half a dozen yachts were tied to the small jetty. It was so calm and peaceful.

She went and sat on a rock and thought about how special this place was. Even if she hadn't spent so much time here in the past, it would still be very special. Turning around, she could see the little church at Monastery Vlaherna. It was such a strange place for a church. Although it was only about twelve foot square, it was so beautiful. Miriam hadn't really appreciated its beauty before, but something was drawing her towards it. She took a deep breath and walked the few metres to the entrance. Inside it was just as she remembered it. For such a small building there were so many pictures on the walls. She took a few euros out of her purse, placed them in a jar and picked up a candle which she lit with another that was burning. She then placed her candle alongside all the others. She stood there quietly taking in the aroma and its peacefulness, yet slowly she could feel the tears coming.

"Oh Rex, I'm so sorry. It should never have happened. All those years I've kept that secret. Please, please, forgive me, Rex."

Miriam felt very lightheaded with her legs turning to jelly. She went to sit in the chair in the corner, took out a bottle of water from her bag, wiped her face, took a few deep breaths and stared at the candle. In all the years of coming to this little church she hadn't ever lit a candle before. That was what all those sleepless nights were about. It was leading her here. Should she have told Rex about what had happened or did he know? They had spent nearly 50 years together. It had been perfect. They loved each other so much, but if she had told him that perfect life would have been ruined. After a few minutes reflecting on this, Miriam felt better. It was time to move on. Time to look to the future. She had laid the past to rest. Stepping out of the church, the heat of the sun immediately hit her and she headed back along the beach. Where did that come from? she thought to herself. I don't think that church has ever come into my mind before. How could one little room with all those pictures make me feel so different?

Miriam walked on until she found herself at a beach café where she ordered half a litre of red wine and spent the next two hours sitting in the shade watching all the families enjoying their time on the beach. It took her right back to their family holidays. As she paid her bill and looked towards the little jetty she could see the water taxi departing. She knew it would be another half an hour for the next one, so she decided to take a short walk along the road behind the beach. The butterflies were now returning. This was the road they had walked along so many times a day, every year they came to Holkamos.

Miriam stopped dead in her tracks. There it was! The house they had rented for 20 years. However, it seemed different now. It didn't look like a holiday let any more, the garden was immaculate. It looked like a private house and the old sign with the rental phone number had disappeared. It was so different and that was good! Very good, because that was the past and this is the future.

As Miriam walked back to the jetty to catch the taxi back to Holkamos harbour she said to herself, "Now I've seen that, all my doubts about coming back here are behind me. I can now start to enjoy the rest of my time here in Greece." Getting on the little boat she wished it was evening and dark because if she had to sum up Holkamos in one snapshot it would be the one coming up. As the taxi left Volmos beach and travelled around the cliff with the castle on top, this was the first view of the harbour from the sea. It was a view like no other and at night looking at all the lights twinkling in the water she closed her eyes and could imagine every detail. Tears rolled down her face. She wasn't sure whether they were tears of happiness or tears of sadness, but it was time to move on and look to the future.

Amy and Heather had a lovely day on the beach. It had been years since they had spent a day relaxing together. It had been a special day for both of them. On the way back to the apartment they stopped at one of the cafes for a cold drink and sitting looking out to sea they both commented on what a special day it had been.

"Mum, it's been lovely today. I've really enjoyed it. Before we came back here I was worried it would be so sad without Grandad. In one way it is, but in another it's as if we are thinking about him more than usual. That's good, don't you think? I miss him so much, but do you know something? If I had a dad in my life I don't think I'd have had such a wonderful relationship with

Grandad. Over the years people have asked me whether I'd like to find out who my father is and what he's up to, but he would just be a stranger to me, not family. I've never felt I've missed out on anything ever. It might be difficult for some people to understand that, but I've had and still have a fabulous life. My family is and has always been you, Nan and Grandad."

"Oh, darling, I'm so lucky you feel like that and I feel exactly the same. If I hadn't got pregnant I would have missed out on something very special, being a mum. That's the most important thing in my life."

"But you would have met someone else, got married and had a family."

"No, Amy. I don't think so. I really don't know where my life would have taken me, but one thing for sure is I wouldn't be as happy as I am now."

They made their way back to the apartment and in the evening went down to one of the restaurants in the harbour. Miriam told them all about the old holiday let and going for a walk but didn't mention anything about going to the old church. That was private. Something she was hoping was now well in the past. Something else slightly worried her though, but she wasn't sure whether it was just her imagination or something she needed to give some thought to. From leaving the apartment to walking along to the restaurant, Amy was looking at the ground rather than in the shop windows. It was if she was trying to hide her face and when they arrived at the restaurant she didn't want to sit in view of people, preferring to be tucked away in the corner. Why was this? What was she afraid of? Could this be something to do with initially not wanting to come on holiday?

Over dinner they planned to get up early the next day and catch the sea taxi over to Volmos. They would have a day lying in the sun and reading. Miriam had suggested they walk over as first thing in the morning it would be cooler, but both Amy and Heather were insistent that they should go by boat.

"But, girls, we used to love that walk. All the little shops on the hill, the beautiful smells of jasmine and the bougainvillea from the top of the hill over Holkamos. If we go by taxi, we'll miss all of that."

"Mum, you're not as young as you were. I think it'll be too much for you. I really think this holiday we should give the hill a miss."

Oh dear. Something wasn't quite right. Perhaps Miriam wasn't the only one who needed to put right the past. Could they all have secrets on this this little Greek island?

Chapter 7

Back in England Paul was lonely and missing Amy even though it had only been a few days. It felt strange not having her around and he was starting to realise the importance of her input in his work. He was good at designing websites, but it was Amy's eye, seeing things from a customer's perspective, that he really needed. She was the one who said whether the way a particular website had been designed would encourage her to buy the product. For the first time ever, a company had rejected his ideas and mock up for their website. Paul knew he had rushed it and failed to give it his full attention, but his mind was elsewhere, on Holkamos. For a start there must be a reason why Miriam insisted they go back but more importantly, what was it with the ring? Over the years he had caught Amy fiddling with it on many occasions, when she had been deep in thought. If only she would be honest with him about it.

Over the next couple of days they followed the same routine. Amy would nip to the bakers, buy a few pastries for breakfast and then they would walk to the harbour to catch the sea taxi to Volmos. They would lie in the sunshine, leave the beach at lunch time and enjoy a Greek salad or a club sandwich. They would then return to the beach until they caught the sea taxi back around 6.30, go back to the apartment, shower, glam themselves up and go out for dinner. They were having such a lovely time.

Miriam was still worried about both Heather and Amy. Amy was still walking around in the evenings as though she was hiding from something, while during the day she wore a big floppy hat disguising her face.

Her excuse was that she didn't want to burn her face in the sun. Whatever was going on in her head was anyone's guess.

They had their lunch in the beach café and had started to walk back to the sun loungers when they noticed the wind had increased and the calm sea had begun to get slightly rougher.

"I think we should call it a day. It looks like it might rain. What do you think, Mum?"

"Yes, I agree. The waves are really getting bigger. Look it's all going over the jetty. Come to think of it, I've not seen the sea taxi for over an hour. Perhaps they've stopped operating as it's too windy."

The look on Heather's face said it all. They would have to walk up the hill to the castle and back down the other side, but because of the situation there were no other options. They gathered their things and set off for the 45-minute walk. Miriam thought that everything in life happens for a reason. Now let's see what happens when we get to the top.

It was a steep hill and Miriam certainly couldn't walk as quickly as she used to, but standing nearly at the top and looking back over Volmos was a view she could never tire of. Apart from a few more apartments and villas in the background, nothing had changed. A bit further on they arrived at the foot of the castle and could see down to Holkamos harbour.

"I've missed you, Holkamos. It's good to be back. It's so lovely to be somewhere so beautiful and safe, not to mention the happy times you've given us. Girls, that's the hard bit done. Now for the easy part, downhill and a peep into the shops."

"Oh, Mum," Amy said, "I forgot all about this little shop. Can you remember if that's the shop where the lady bought jewellery from you? She was so nice and she sold it within a day. I wish we had thought about it, you could have brought some from home. I bet she would have bought the lot. Can we go in?"

"No, I don't think so. Let's get back to the apartment before it rains. She might not be there anymore. Oh, come on. Let's treat ourselves to some more cakes from the bakery."

Now this is what it's all about. It's something to do with this shop. To be honest, I can't even remember it. Why doesn't Heather want to go near it? What happened? This holiday is certainly ruffling a few feathers. Amy's acting as if she's in hiding and something has really upset Heather.

"We've got time. It looks like the clouds are pacing over. Come on, Amy. Let's go in. Are you coming, Heather?"

They all went in the little shop, although Miriam wasn't at all interested in any of the stock. She just wanted to see Heather's reaction.

"Good afternoon. What a lovely shop. I'm so glad you're still here. We came many years ago and you bought some of my mum's jewellery from her. Oh, it is you. You're wearing one of her pendants."

"Hello, and welcome back to Holkamos. Please feel free to browse around. I just need to pop out into the back. Please excuse me."

Miriam sensed a difficult situation. The woman was upset and she could tell she was about to cry. Heather went as white as a sheet and looked like she was going to be sick. Amy hadn't noticed as she was busy looking around, but now wasn't the time to be browsing. It was time to leave. This whole situation needed to be discussed.

"Thank you, but I think it's going to rain. We'd best get a move on. Come on, Amy. Heather, thank you. We'll pop back another day. We still have next week. Goodbye."

They walked down the rest of the hill in silence, stopped off at the bakery and then returned to the apartment. Miriam made an excuse to go and rest and Amy said that she was going to read in her room. Once both of them had gone, Heather poured herself a glass of wine, drank it straight down and then poured a second glass, which she took out on the balcony.

This wasn't meant to happen, she thought to herself. What do I do? I'm scared, so very scared and I can't talk about it. I don't even want to think about it. Bloody Greece. Why now and why me? What do I do? I need to be strong? Come on, Heather. Pull yourself together.

Five hours later they were ready to go out and the conversation had returned to a more normal one. What are you wearing? Where shall we go to eat? There was just one difference. Heather could see her mother looking at her differently. It wasn't in a bad way, but in a loving, caring, motherly way. I just want her to hold me and tell me everything's going to be okay, she thought.

They all went off and had a lovely meal with perhaps a little too much wine, but that helped. The evening was exactly the same as the others had been, laughing and joking together, but both Heather and Miriam knew that the events of the day needed to be resolved or at least discussed.

Holkamos, what are you doing to my family, thought Miriam. What are we hiding from? You are the secrets, the reason we've not been here for ten years. Perhaps now it's time to let them out so they can fly and be free.

Chapter 8

"Good morning, Mum. Did you sleep well? It's nine-thirty."

"Oh yes, I must have. I blame the wine! What a lovely evening we had. Is Amy up yet?"

"You've just missed her. She's nipped to the bakery."

"She's a good girl. I'm so lucky to have such a lovely granddaughter and a very special daughter. You know that, don't you, Heather? I'm so proud of you and what you've achieved in life. As for your dad, never a day went by when he didn't say how lucky he was to have such a loving and caring daughter. I'm so glad we've come back to Holkamos. I think it's something I should have done a long time ago but was frightened to own up to.

"You know, Heather, things in life happen for a reason. We all make mistakes along the way. I know, but I've had to move on and forget them. Opportunities also come up and if the time and the situation are right we must grab them with both hands and just go for it as long as it's not hurting anyone. We only get one chance to live our life and I really believe we should make the most of it. Coming back to Greece has really made me think about things. I love you very much, Heather, and there's nothing you could ever do to change that. You know that, don't you?"

"Amy, is that you? It is! Please stop."

Amy froze. It was the voice she was dreading, the voice she was praying never to hear again. "Keep walking," she said to herself. "He'll go away. What do I say? Don't make a fool of yourself. Just smile and say hello. Come on, Amy, put on an act."

"Hello, Andréas."

"Please speak. This isn't nice." Oh God, he's got tears in his eyes. Say something. What's he doing? He's lifting his hand up. He's still wearing that ring after all these years. I'm still part of his life. He's seen my ring. Please don't cry. He turned and walked away. Amy took some deep breaths.

Come on. Pretend it didn't happen, she thought. He knows you're on the island now and obviously didn't want to talk. That's it. Move on.

"So, darling, what delights have you brought back from the bakery today? Are you okay? You look a little flushed."

"Yes, it's really hot out there today. I think we might have to spend some time in the shade."

The three of them sat on the balcony eating their pastries, drinking coffee, chatting about events down in the harbour and planning their day. Miriam suggested that they didn't have to spend all day together. She was more than happy to be by herself. She thought she might just go down to the town beach for a change and she also wanted to get some postcards. The other two laughed and commented on whether people still send postcards. Perhaps Miriam should just make an Instagram account and then everyone could see what's she was doing.

Miriam also said that as she'd been out and had a lot to eat and drink over the past couple of nights, she'd prefer to have an evening in, if they didn't mind.

"I think once I come off the beach and buy my postcards, I'll stop somewhere and have an omelette. Just something light. So, feel free to do whatever today. Shall we say meet back here for breakfast tomorrow?"

With that Miriam went to get ready. Amy said she thought she might have a lie down for a while. She wanted to give the sunshine a break today. That just left Heather to plan her day. What was she going to do? She knew what she should do and had been awake most of the night thinking about it, but deep down she just wanted to run away.

"I'll walk down to the harbour with you, Mum. I might just take a look at the boat trips."

Once down in the harbour Heather realised she'd left it too late to book a day trip as they'd already left, so she walked with Miriam towards the town beach. As they turned the corner there was the little train. It was called a train, but it was more like a few little square boxes with seats in, a toy train.

"That's what I'll do. I'll get the little train up to Creakos, Mum. Have a lovely day."

"And you, darling. Please don't worry about me. Go and have some fun."

The little train was packed with four people in each carriage. Off it went, stopping at the watermill so people could have a look in the museum and take photos, and then up to the village of Creakos. It was hot, so Heather headed for one of the cafés. Sitting under a lemon tree in the shade she had a frappe and watched the world go by.

Miriam was the complete opposite. She was determined to top up her tan. She found a sun lounger, got out her book and settled there for the day.

Heather sat for an hour chatting to other holiday makers about Holkamos and how many years she'd been coming for holidays. She then had a little walk around. Not a lot had changed, there were just a few more modern restaurants. She was wondering how to spend the rest of the day when she could hear someone calling her.

"Miss Heather, Miss Heather. Hello. Welcome. Oh, it's so lovely to see you. So many years and so much has happened. Where is Miss Miriam, Mr Rex and baby Amy? I expect baby Amy is all grown up."

"Hello, Carolina. It's good to see you. How are all the family?"

"Please come to my house and tell me what's been happening. I'll show you photos and you can meet my grandchildren."

Heather went back to Carolina's house and met the two grandchildren and Andréas' wife, Katia. She explained how they had sold the two adjoining houses and moved there. It was very wet and damp down in Volmos during the winter and once her husband had died they needed the money. So now she helped take care of the grandchildren so that Andréas and Katia could work the season. Heather explained how Rex had died and that this was their first time back for ten years. Carolina insisted on giving Heather a meal and the afternoon flew by. She was so pleased Heather had come up to the village and they made arrangements to all meet up. Phone numbers were exchanged and Heather said her goodbyes.

"Oh, Miss Heather, I forgot to tell you who bought the houses from us. It was Mr and Mrs Docking. You remember Melvin and Pearle, the couple who were always here the same time as you. Sadly, Pearle died, so Melvin lives there by himself now. His family visit and he rents the other house out. I'm sure he would like to see you all."

How lovely is that, Heather was thinking, as she made her way back to where the train turned around for the return journey to Holkamos. She couldn't wait to tell Miriam and Amy all the news, especially Amy, as she had played with Andréas every summer since she was a toddler. What a lovely afternoon she'd had. It had taken her mind off the things that were worrying her. The late afternoon sun was still very hot and as the train approached the town, Heather decided to get off and stroll back to the apartment.

She found herself standing at the foot of the castle looking over the town. The restaurants were starting to prepare for dinner and staff were arriving for their duties. It was those few hours where Holkamos changed from a beach resort to a twinkling harbour of bars and restaurants. Heather loved to watch the transformation from day to night. She walked to the first restaurant which overlooked the harbour and ordered a glass of wine. The perfect end to such a lovely day.

An hour or so later and a couple more glasses of wine, Holkamos was alive with people choosing a restaurant for the evening. Everyone was dressed up and lights twinkled. What more could anyone want? Heather considered herself fortunate. She paid her bill and started to make her way back to the apartment, but that meant going down the hill. The little shops were busy. A few more yards and she would be at Edelina's. Heather stopped suddenly. What should she do? She was excited, but her heart was beating fast and she felt confident. Here goes, she thought. It's something I have to do and like Mum said, for some strange reason we've had to come back to Holkamos. As she got closer, her nervousness faded.

"Hello, Edelina."

"Hello, Heather."

"How are you? I'm so very sorry for upsetting you yesterday. That wasn't how it should have happened. I've gone over this situation so many times in the last ten years."

"So have I. I've never stopped thinking about you and I truly believed that you'd come back when the time was right."

With that two women came in and asked to try on some clothes. As the shop was so small, Edelina showed Heather to the workroom and told her that she wouldn't be long.

Heather had been in there once before, the day she had brought the jewellery up for Edelina to look at. It seemed as though it was only yesterday. She and Amy had come in browsing and chatted with Edelina who had asked where Heather's necklace was from. Amy pitched in saying that her mother made them. That's when Edelina had asked whether she would make some for her to sell. They agreed that Heather would bring some more to show her the following day. Heather had taken all her and Miriam's necklaces, bracelets and earrings back to the shop. They spread all the items out on the table and discussed prices. Heather had agreed to leave the items with her for the rest of the holiday to see if they would sell and about two weeks later when she returned, Edelina was so excited to have sold everything apart from one pendant that she herself was wearing. She poured them a glass of wine to celebrate their success and talked about Heather sending over some more from England. That's when it happened. Edelina leaned towards Heather and kissed her. It wasn't a peck on the check like two friends would kiss, but one on the lips and they held each other for what seemed like ages. Heather was confused. Never in her life had she felt like this about a man or a woman. What was happening? She pulled away and apologised. Edelina explained there was nothing to apologies for, but Heather was scared. She wanted to run. She had to get out as she didn't need anyone in her life. She could still hear Edelina saying that everything was alright and begging her not to leave. Heather had left though, and that was the very last time she had seen Edelina until yesterday.

The two women tried on nearly everything in the shop but did buy a few things. "Look, we need to talk," said Edelina. "What if I close early, get something to eat and open a bottle of wine? I need to explain what happened. The last thing I wanted to do was upset you. I'm so sorry, Heather. Can we just talk?"

"You don't need to explain anything. That was a long time ago, but I would like to have a glass of wine with you and talk about the jewellery. That would be nice. I'll just text Miriam and Amy and let them know I'll be back later."

Heather helped Edelina bring the stock in from outside the shop and chatted about the clothes as they did so. Once everything was locked up they went upstairs to the flat. Edelina opened the balcony doors, giving a view of the harbour in the distance and the mountains. There was just enough room for a little table, two chairs and a couple of plant pots containing some beautiful Bizzy Lizzies. Heather sat down and Edelina poured the wine.

"Do you like pasta, Heather?"

"Yes, that would be lovely. What a fabulous view you have."

Edelina explained that was why she had bought the property. They both sat and chatted for a while before preparing the pasta. Edelina told Heather about her life and how she had left a stressful job in Germany. One day while on the train to the centre of Berlin, she thought to herself, How many more years can I continue doing this? By the time she had got off the train she had decided to give it all up and move to Greece. She didn't have a clue how that would happen and what she would do when she moved, but the deadline was set. After three months' notice her days of commuting would be over. She explained how she'd never looked back as she had such a wonderful, peaceful and healthy life here.

They continued to chat from the open plan kitchen / lounge. Heather talked about her jewellery and the craft markets she attended and also that because she was self-employed and worked from home she could split her days up by doing accounting and book work two days a week and then jewellery making for three or four days. She was very lucky. The pasta was lovely and sitting overlooking Holkamos was a thing to be cherished. There was no mention of the kiss.

Edelina asked about Amy and Heather was very open and honest. She explained that she was very young at the time and was at university. A group of friends had been out for a few drinks and one thing had led to another. Heather had ended up having sex with a lad. It was her first time, she was drunk and all she could remember about it was that it wasn't at all enjoyable. When she discovered she was pregnant, her parents were wonderful about it. Their response was that no one had died and Heather had given them a grandchild. As a family they would work through it together and that's exactly what had happened. There was no shame or disappointment to any of it. She had been so lucky. Amy didn't know who her dad was and wasn't bothered about finding him. As far as she was concerned, she had raised Amy with the help of Miriam and Rex.

"It's getting late and I need to be going. Thank you so much for a lovely evening. I've enjoyed it so much and I'm so sorry about last time. It was nothing to do with you, just me and my stupidity. Since that night at university twenty odd years ago, there's been no one else, not even a one-night stand."

"Thank you for a lovely evening too and I hope we can do it again before you leave. We also need to talk about jewellery."

Edelina led Heather back down through the shop and they said their good nights. Heather turned to Edelina, thanked her again and kissed her goodnight on the cheek.

It was about a 15 minute walk back to the apartment and Heather was so happy. She felt different, a feeling she had never experienced before. It sounded stupid, but her whole body felt loose and free. She wanted to dance, run and skip. Things she hadn't done since her school days. She was happy. No, not just happy, she was contented.

*

Back on Volmos Melvin was sitting in his beautiful garden. He could hear the young family next door but couldn't understand what they were saying as he didn't speak the language. It was obvious to him that they were happy and it took him right back to the first time he and Pearle were here with their son. It was the first holiday abroad with him, and Carolina and her husband had been so kind to them. That was the start of this special relationship with Holkamos. Melvin poured himself another glass of wine and moved under the olive tree which kept so many memories. How many nights he and Pearle had sat there laughing and joking with Rex, Miriam and Carolina, watching the three children running around and playing together and Andréas teaching the other two Greek. As they got older, he taught them rude words but they didn't understand them. The three children were so close for that short time every year.

It was such a strange situation. For six weeks every summer these three families did everything together, eat, drink, go to the beach, have fabulous evenings in Holkamos town and then once the time was up they'd go their separate ways until the following year. Oh, how he would just love to enjoy one of those days again. He missed the company so much. Life was good when he was busy doing things, but in the evenings when he was by himself, he felt so lonely.

Chapter 9

They were all up early the next morning. Amy was back with the pastries and Heather told them about her dinner with Edelina, how she was going to supply her with jewellery once they had sorted out the logistics and that she was very excited about it. Miriam talked about her day and how she and Amy had a quiet night in.

"Oh, I nearly forgot. Guess where I spent yesterday afternoon? I bumped into Carolina and went back to her home in Creakos to meet Andréas' wife, Katia, and their two children; it was lovely. Carolina told me how they sold the two houses when her husband died and that's why they've moved up the hill. I didn't see Andréas as he was working in his uncle's restaurant down in the harbour, but you'll never guess who bought Carolina's two houses. It's such a small world. It was Melvin and Pearle! Sadly, Pearle died but Melvin lives in one house and rents the other one out."

No sooner had she told them this than the atmosphere changed. It was like looking at two ghosts. Colour drained first from Amy's face and then Miriam looked quite ill.

"Are you alright, Mum? You really don't look well."

"No, darling. I'm not feeling too good. It's come on suddenly. I think I've got a bit of a funny tummy. Please excuse me."

Heather was confused. One minute they were chatting away happily, the next it was like someone had died. She made another coffee and went back onto the balcony; it was more than half an hour before she saw either her mother or Amy. Miriam came out first and said that she was going back to bed and then Amy appeared shortly afterwards, casually yet smartly dressed, with her hair and make-up done. Not a bit like her for the day time.

"Mum, I thought I'd go and have a look around the shops today, if that's okay with you. I'm not in the mood for the beach. I'll see you back here later. Bye."

What was all that about? Heather wondered. It looks like I've got the day to myself. She had a shower, spending more time than usual on her appearance. She went through all her jewellery and picked out everything she had made. It would be the perfect excuse to go back and see Edelina. When she was ready she left a note for Miriam and off she went.

No sooner had the door closed than Miriam was out of the bedroom and sitting on the balcony, thinking things through. She couldn't help but think about all those weeks of not being able to sleep properly. It was horrible and the last thing she wanted to happen was to go back to England and have that start up again. She had never been one to run away from a situation or problem and she had mentally made her peace with Rex.

Amy was on a mission. There was no hiding for her today. She felt good and had done nothing wrong. Her life was perfect. Paul loved every bone in her body, they had a successful business between them and she was happy. As she made her way down the little windy streets, stopping to look in shop windows, she was also checking her appearance. Once down in the harbour she walked along by the sea wall and past the restaurants where the staff were busy preparing for the day's business. Amy reached the end and turned to walk back. The sun was shining and Amy felt good. It wasn't long before her mission was accomplished.

"Hello, Amy. I'm sorry about the other day, it was such a shock to see you. I didn't know what to think."

"It's lovely to see you as well, Andréas. I expect

Carolina told you that my mum had lunch with her yesterday."

"Yes, but, Amy, we need to talk. I want to explain things to you. I want to apologise."

"You've nothing to apologise for, but I'd like to talk to you about my life in England."

"That would be nice. How about if I ask my uncle for some time off and we meet for a coffee or a walk. If you let me have your number. I'll text you later."

They exchanged numbers, Andréas went back to work and Amy carried on walking along the prom. That went alright, she thought to herself. Awkwardness had disappeared. They were just two friends catching up on each other's news.

Heather made her way up to Edelina's shop, excited to be seeing her again. As she made her way through the town she stopped and bought some sweet and savoury pastries from the bakery and a bunch of wild flowers from an old Greek lady who was sitting on a little stool outside a small house.

"Good morning. I thought I'd bring some of my jewellery to show you, that's if you've got a few minutes to spare. These flowers are for you, as a thank you for last night, it was so lovely. I really enjoyed myself. Oh, and I stopped off at the bakery as well."

"Thank you. We'll have plenty of time as everyone's on the beach as it's so hot. I'll make us a coffee. It's so nice to see you again, Heather. I was hoping you'd pop in today."

Back at the apartment Miriam was getting herself ready. She too was on a mission and just like Amy and Heather she was making a special effort to look nice. Today she was wearing a lovely summer dress that she had bought when shopping with Amy. Miriam had thought it was a bit too young for her at first, but now here in the Greek sunshine it looked fine. She was very happy with how she scrubbed up.

Back at the shop Heather and Edelina were having a lovely time putting necklaces with different tops and discussing fashion; it was a day spent on the shop. Edelina was so pleased to have a fresh pair of eyes helping her change the stock around and matching outfits together. She had never had this before and it was exciting bouncing ideas off each other.

Amy's phone rang. It was Andréas telling her that his uncle needed some supplies from Preveza and asking whether she would like to go with him to get them. Perhaps they could stop and have a drink on the way. Amy thought it was a good idea and they planned to meet near the taxi rank.

Just like the other two, Miriam was also checking her appearance in the shop windows as she made her way down to the harbour. She felt very confident, but that was nothing new as she had always been an optimistic character. When she got to the sea taxi she realised that she'd just missed one. As she waited for the next, she could see Amy walking away from the harbour and what a different Amy it was. Her head was held high and she also looked very confident. Miriam watched Amy until she was out of sight, and it crossed her mind how neither Heather nor Amy had wanted to come back to Holkamos but now they both seemed so very happy. This wasn't a normal holiday. The atmosphere was strange for all three of them. The sea taxi pulled into the jetty, a few people got off and then the driver helped the queue of people to get on. The sea was so calm and off they sailed towards Volmos.

Andréas met Amy and they drove away from the town

to catch the ferry. He explained that they would need to go straight to Preveza as the cash and carry closed at midday for a siesta. A friend of his had a little beach restaurant near to the ferry port in a little cove where they could stop for a drink on the way back.

The sea taxi pulled in to Volmos and Miriam made her away across the busy beach to the little road that led to Creakos. She brushed the sand from her feet and passed the little beach shop. Once more she checked her appearance in the window and smiled to herself, thinking how vain she was. Forgetting that the road was very narrow, she had to let cars and delivery vehicles pass by her. Families were coming in the opposite direction all very excited to be heading for the beach. There were holiday apartments and houses on both sides plus a few little grocery shops with restaurants on the side. As the road wound around, it brought back so many memories as this was the way they would all come back from town. In those days they very rarely caught the sea taxi. They would walk back up the steep hill to the castle and then down on to Volmos, walking their heavy meals off. Sometimes it would be just the four of them and other times there might be a larger group who had all made friends on that holiday. They were special times and Miriam often wondered whether friendships like these could be made elsewhere, or was it that Holkamos was such a magical special place?

A little further on she turned the corner and there were the cottages, looking a lot fresher with their new paint, but the welcoming appearance was still the same. For some strange reason Miriam wasn't at all nervous. She felt as if she was coming home to somewhere she had missed for a long while. Walking up the path, she noticed that someone was at home as the shutters were open. She knocked on the door, which in itself was strange, as normally she would have just unlocked it.

The door opened and it felt like going back in time. There he was. It had been ten years, but he hadn't changed one bit!

"Hello, Miriam. What a lovely surprise! Are you by yourself or is the family with you? Please come in."

Melvin led her through the house and into the back garden. She could see that the house had been decorated and looked completely different. She was pleased about that as she wanted to keep her memories. The last thing she wanted was for it to be completely the same with Rex missing. She would have felt lost and empty without him. Melvin pointed to a lovely little shady terrace which was also new. She sat there while Melvin went to get them both a drink and couldn't believe how much the garden had changed. It was now a cross between an English country garden and a Mediterranean one, with lots of tall palms and olive trees, cosmos and geraniums underneath. It was so peaceful and relaxing. Melvin returned with a bottle of wine.

"Your garden is magnificent. I can't believe how it's changed. You've worked so hard. I remember it full of children's toys and a climbing frame. This it is just stunning."

Melvin then told Miriam the story of how his garden came into being and also the reason why he was now living on the island.

"You see, Miriam, when we came back from Rex's funeral, Pearle and I decided that it was about time we thought about our future. We were both around the same age as you and Rex and it could easily have been one of us rather than him. I decided to take early retirement and we came out here for a week's holiday in the May, a completely different time of the year for us. The weather was good. It wasn't too hot, but warm enough to still be outdoors all day. We had such a lovely time and we both said how it would be so nice to be here for longer and wondered whether we really could do it. After talking it over with our son and his wife they suggested that perhaps we should buy something small in the UK and something here too.

"I won't bore you with the fine details, but we sold our home in London, had my son's garage converted into a little granny annexe and then came out to look for a property here. By chance, Carolina was selling both these properties. We only wanted one, but she wanted to sell both and would not separate them, so we ended up buying both. It was good in a way because while we were decorating one, we could live in the other. Some people talk about the nightmares of purchasing property abroad, but we didn't experience any problems at all. Everything from the purchase to builders and plumbers went so smoothly. We were so lucky. Let me get you another glass of wine. I won't be a minute."

Miriam could not get over how positive Melvin was. He hadn't mentioned Pearle's death yet and it did need to be talked about. The garden must keep him very busy and renting the other house would also be a lot of work. Melvin talked as fast as an express train. Miriam could hardly get a word in.

"So, where did I get to, Miriam? Oh yes, so both houses were ready and we started renting the other one out. The first two years were lovely. We had so many great guests staying from May to October but towards the end of that second season Pearle wasn't feeling too well. We were going back to England in November for a few months so once back and several doctor appointments and hospital visits later, the worse was confirmed. Pearle had cancer. It was diagnosed on the fifth of December and she died two months later, on the fifth of February. It was all so quick."

"Oh, Melvin. I'm so very sorry. I really don't know what to say."

"Those two months should have been devastating, but they weren't. As a family we all pulled together and I know it sounds odd, but they were full of fun and laughter. The grandchildren, despite being so young, understood and there wasn't a day went by where they didn't have Pearle laughing. Three days before she died we were in my son's house. The dining room was her bedroom. It overlooked the garden. The room was full of family photos and children's toys. Everyone was out, even the nurses who called in several times a day weren't there. It was just the two of us. I went to make a cup of tea and when I came back Pearle said that we needed to talk. She asked me what would happen if the roles were reversed and it was me dying? What would I be saying to her? Oh, Miriam, I couldn't reply, and she knew it so she answered instead. "You would be telling me not to mope around, get back to Volmos, earn a living from the house and enjoy the sunshine." She made me promise to do just that. It wasn't something I felt good about as it was our dream, but she too would be part of it. Miriam, she knew she was dying and once I had made this promise, her health deteriorated quickly and three days later she died."

"What can I say? You've kept your promise. You've created a lovely home and garden."

"Oh, the garden wasn't like this. It was the one job we hadn't done. To be honest, we hadn't even talked about it. This is the garden I created for her. It's the only thing that's kept me sane for the last six years. If I didn't have this garden, I'd have drunk myself into an early grave here in the sunshine."

"You should be very proud of yourself, Melvin. Knowing Pearle, she would have been over the moon with it."

"Now all of that's off my chest, I'll let you get a word in. I'm sorry I've gone on for so long, but I'm not very good at stopping when I've started. I want to hear all about Heather and Amy, but first how do you fancy a club sandwich?"

"That would be very nice. Would you like some help?"

"No, you sit there and enjoy the garden."

On the ferry heading to Preveza the conversation was all very positive. Amy told Andréas all about her social media business, the companies she promoted on Facebook and Twitter, Paul's web design business and what her mum and nan were up to. It was a very happy picture with everything apart from roses around the door. Amy was feeling good. They were adults now. Previously they were just two kids without any experience of life.

Once off the ferry they made the short drive to the warehouse. Amy stayed in the van while Andréas got what he needed for his uncle. It was the perfect opportunity for Amy to Tweet and Facebook for the companies she was promoting. Paul had sent her a text to see if she was free to chat, but as she didn't think the time was right she ignored the text. That could wait until the van was loaded up. They then made their way back to catch the return ferry.

"Are you sure you want to stop for a drink? We can go straight back if you'd prefer?"

"No, it would be nice, if you don't need to rush back."

"I've plenty of time. I don't need to be back for at least four hours."

Andréas turned left down a windy road until he got to the water's edge. "There it is, Nico's lovely beach restaurant. Come on. I'll introduce you to him."

They walked over to the restaurant. Nico seemed to already know about Amy. He said it was so nice to meet her at last. She didn't really have time to ponder on that, as the place was quite busy. Andréas went behind the bar and brought out two bottles of beer.

"Come on. It's busy here. Let's go and sit on the rocks."

"This is a lovely place. I've never been here before."

"We locals keep it a secret. It's quiet but still busy enough to have a lovely atmosphere. Amy, I'm so sorry about you know what. It just happened. You were in England. It was winter here and one thing led to another with Katia."

"We were kids, only seventeen, living thousands of miles apart. It was never going to come to anything. We both knew that it was all about the summer, having fun. We played together as young children."

"I know, but we..."

"Well, we sort of... It was your first time and mine. Neither of us knew what we were doing and it should have been a special thing, but it was clumsy and like I said we were kids."

"But I wanted it to be special and if only we had a few more days together it would have been. I loved you so much and I wanted you to love me."

"Oh, I loved you and because we both lost our virginity together I loved you even more. Anyway, Andréas, that's all in the past. You've got your wife and lovely children and I've got Paul. We can still be friends. We might have only seen each other for six weeks every year, but we grew up together."

"I know, Amy, but I still love you."

With that he went to get some more beers. Amy didn't feel the same about Andréas. Although she didn't love him, she did fancy him and that could be a problem. When he returned he looked as though he'd been crying. This was getting awkward.

"Come on. Let's go for a walk. Show me around this beautiful cove."

They walked back towards the van but took a turning to the left through a wooded area with lots of olive trees with bundles of nets all ready to spread around the trees. It was a lot cooler now. Andréas led the way; it was all up and down through the trees and Amy could just about see the sea. Finally they came to the edge. There it was, the sea but no beach – just the wide open ocean in all its glory and not a person or a manmade item in sight. Paradise!

Amy put her hand into his and as he turned to face her she could feel their nervousness. I think perhaps this is the time to do it right, don't you? Their kiss lasted for ages and then Amy started to undo his shirt and before long they were naked. There was no fumbling or wondering what they should be doing. This time it was beautiful. Amy had waited so long for this, all those years of wanting him and even in her wildest dreams she could never have imagined just how good it could be. It was over so quickly and they lay there in each other's arms saying nothing until finally they dressed in silence and walked back to the van. The short journey back to Holkamos town seemed to take ages. You could cut the atmosphere with a knife.

"Where would you like me to drop you off?"

"Anywhere. I need to get some shopping in the town."

Andréas pulled up in the taxi rank. They smiled a smile of happiness rather than one of guilt. As Amy got out the van she blew him a kiss, a kiss that said so much.

Miriam and Melvin had a lovely lunch and she filled him in on what Heather and Amy were up to. She tried to explain about the social media business but neither of them really understood how it worked. Melvin talked about his son and grandchildren. It was a lovely afternoon, two friends catching up on old times.

"Was what happened all those years ago between us wrong, Melvin? Are we now paying the price for our guilt? Did Pearle and Rex ever find out?"

"It wasn't planned, Miriam. I was working from here

for the summer and was on a tight schedule. The work had to be done. Everyone was going to the Greek night up in Creakos and you didn't want to go. We stopped and had a drink, passion took over and we made love. It was just the once. It was like something I had never experienced before or since. May I say we weren't in love or having an affair. It was pure lust and no one got hurt. That's not to say that I haven't thought about it over the years, but it happened. If we had confessed, two families would have suffered so much pain. We couldn't have done that to them."

"But we shouldn't have done it. It was wrong."

"Did you love Rex any less, because I still loved Pearle as much after as I did before? Look, Miriam, we could debate this until the cows come home. It happened. It was very special, but that's as far as it goes. We've had a lovely time together today. I think what happened all those years ago should be left where it was, in the past."

The subject was then dropped. Melvin wanted to know when the three of them could come for dinner. He couldn't wait to catch up with Heather and Amy and so a date was arranged. Melvin insisted on cooking dinner for them all. It would be like old times, all of them back here on Volmos. He then walked Miriam back to the sea taxi. Her head was spinning. She knew what happened all those years ago was wrong, but it was too late to put it right now. Both Rex and Pearle were no longer here. The last thing they needed to do was tell their children. Perhaps it was time to leave it where it belonged – in the past.

Chapter 10

What a day yesterday had been for all three of them. Last night's dinner was in a lovely restaurant overlooking Volmos, close to the castle. Most of it had been spent in silence, although not in a bad way. Heather had talked about Edelina's shop, how she had helped move stock around and the pieces of jewellery she was going to send over. Miriam could see such a difference in her daughter. Heather was always a very positive person. She never moaned or complained, but now it was as if she was on fire with excitement. Miriam was so happy for her. This was what she and Rex had wished for Heather and Miriam sensed this was the start of something very special.

Amy told them about her day and how she'd had a lovely walk. She mentioned that she had bumped into Andréas briefly, but that was all. The main conversation was about Miriam's day with Melvin. All three of them were looking forward to going to the old holiday house for dinner, but the plans for today were to take the little boat to Newtonos.

It had been many years since they had been to Newtonos beach. Amy couldn't even remember going there. They got three sunbeds and stayed there until their lunch of Greek salads with hot bread and a bottle of white wine. Back on the sunbeds for the afternoon rays, this was a real holiday day. Sea, sunshine and books. Although all three of them gave the impression they were having a good time when secretly they all wished they were somewhere else.

Back at the apartment while getting ready to go out, Amy suggested that perhaps they could go and eat in Andréas' uncle's restaurant that night. After having said that, Amy wondered whether it was a good thing or not, but it was too late now. Miriam and Heather were looking forward to it and couldn't wait to see Andréas. It was a lovely evening with a warm breeze. They stopped just as they got to the harbour for Amy to send Andréas a text saying they were coming and that she had mentioned bumping into him.

"It's still early. Why don't we have a pre-dinner drink in one of these bars? I love to sit and watch the town come alive at night. What do you say, Mum?"

"That would be lovely. Are you alright with that, Amy?"

Amy agreed, although she wasn't sure about it. All she wanted to do was see Andréas. She could smell him and the feel of his hands on her body were still in her mind. Another half hour wouldn't matter, but had she been stupid suggesting it in the first place? Andréas would be there waiting on tables and they would make it worse. There wouldn't be any contact between them. Oh, God, Amy, you do get yourself into a muddle sometimes.

Gin and tonics over. They were off to the restaurant.

"Oh, there he is. Look how grown up he is. Well, I suppose having a family does that to you."

"Hello. Oh, Miriam and Heather. It's so good to see you again after all these years. Hello again, Amy. Please come in. I have a lovely table here right on the front. You'll be able to see the boats coming and going."

While they sat, Andréas quickly returned with three glasses of ouzo and the menus. Amy felt sick. What was she gaining from being here? Her initial idea was that she wanted to see Andréas, but now she realised it was a stupid idea. She just wanted to go back to the apartment, but that wasn't going to happen. Something else was also annoying her. Heather had been texting for the last hour. If she had been doing that, her mum would have commented. The whole evening was a disaster.

Andréas had recommended the feta cheese in filo pastry covered in honey and sesame seeds for the starter with sea bass for the main course. The meal was wonderful and eventually Amy began to relax every time Andréas passed by. As he waited on the other tables, he would give her a little smile. Oh, how her heart fluttered. She wanted him so badly, but she realised that would never happen. He worked seven nights a week and when he wasn't in the restaurant, he was with his family.

Once more Heather got her phone out and now this was even getting on Miriam's nerves. Heather was acting out of character and kept apologising, giving the excuse that it was one of her clients who had to take out a loan and she was helping him sort out the paperwork. Neither Amy nor Miriam believed her as she was looking around as though she were looking for someone. It was all most strange.

"Right, Mum and Nan. Shall we make a move?"

"Yes, if you're ready, darling."

"Oh, do you mind if we have a coffee? It's still quite early."

"You've just had a coffee, Mum. Is there something wrong? You seem to be on edge."

"No, I'm fine. I'd just like another coffee."

Andréas was just putting the coffee down when Amy heard a familiar voice and this certainly wasn't the time or the place to be hearing it.

"Hello, ladies. Can I join you?"

"Oh, my God! What a lovely surprise! It's Paul. So, Heather, that's what all that business with your phone was all about."

"Don't I get a kiss, Amy? By the look on your face, I'd settle for a smile. You'd think someone had just died."

"I'm sorry. It's just a bit of a shock, that's all."

"I'm not here to spoil your girly holiday. I'm only

staying for three days, but I thought I should see what this special island was all about. Excuse me, waiter. Is there any chance of getting some food?"

"How rude of me, Paul. Let me introduce you to Andréas. He was a very close family friend. He and Amy played together since they were young children. Andréas, this is Amy's boyfriend, Paul."

With the introductions over, Paul got stuck into some pasta and a pint of beer. Heather explained that she hadn't known about this until late the previous night. It was a spur of the moment thing. Andréas had stopped smiling, Amy felt like her life had come to an end and Miriam realised that perhaps Paul coming wasn't a good idea, but at least it was only for three days.

Back at the apartment Heather moved into Miriam's room so that Amy and Paul could have the other one.

"It's such a shame it's a twin room, Amy, with two single beds, but it could be fun. Let's get in one together. Oh, I've missed not having you in bed with me."

"No, don't be silly. Mum and Nan are only in the next room."

"That's never worried you before. It seems like you're not happy that I've turned up. I feel as if you don't want me here."

"Don't be silly. Of course I'm glad you're here. It's just a bit of a shock, that's all. We can have a nice day together tomorrow."

"Just one thing, Amy. I noticed that the waiter had the same silly ring that you wear. Is there something special about them here in Holkamos? Goodnight."

Chapter 11

It was another beautiful August morning and Melvin was up extra early. He loved to be out and about before it got too busy. As he walked towards the beach the locals were doing their chores before it got too hot. Some mornings Melvin took a short cut through one of the apartment block gardens, but today he decided to walk through the little wooded area and get to the beach from the opposite direction. It was quite cool underneath the olive trees. Walking past the plantations full of tomato and cucumber plants that an old man was watering and then seeing the beach in front of him, Melvin stopped and took in the view. Several yachts were making their way out of the little cove where they'd been moored for the night, out for an adventure around the Greek islands. How exciting!

As Melvin got to the beach he turned right over the little wooden bridge. He could see a few holiday makers putting their towels down and getting ready for a day of sunbathing. A few locals were having a swim before going off for a long day's work. Melvin thought about how much he enjoyed his early morning walks. He loved his walks whatever time of day it was. He was so lucky to live in such a beautiful place.

Once over the bridge there it was, so small and if it wasn't for the cross on the roof it would look like a little stone hut, but once through the little doorway the magnificence and beauty of the Monastery Vlaherna church took his breath away. He stood and took it all in just like he had done every morning since Pearle had died, but as he lit a candle today it felt very different. At first he thought it was guilt, although he had nothing to feel guilty about. His love for Pearle was as strong as it had been since the day they had met. Nothing in the world could ever replace that but something had changed. For the first time since losing Pearle he was starting to feel like he was living rather than just existing. Seeing Miriam again had changed everything.

Amy was up first the next morning. She couldn't wait to get out of the bedroom and sit on the balcony with a coffee. She blamed her nan for all of this. If she hadn't had the stupid idea to come back to Holkamos everything would be normal. Why hadn't they gone somewhere else? This was the past and everyone knows you can't recreate the past. Life changes, people change. What a mess it was.

"Morning, darling. You don't seem very happy about Paul coming. You do know that it was nothing to do with me. The first I heard of it was that he'd booked the ticket and was on his way. Anyway, things could be worse. Why don't you two go off and have a nice day?"

"Why, oh why, did we ever come back here, Mum? I know we loved the place and all three of us have very happy memories here with Grandad, but it's changed."

"No, Amy. It hasn't changed. That's the beauty of Holkamos. Apart from a few new buildings and restaurants with different names, it's still the place we always loved coming to. We've all changed. Nan no longer has Grandad. You've gone from a teenager to a young woman with her own business and I've changed too. After all these years of working hard pleasing my clients and worrying about everything and everyone, perhaps it's time I stood back and looked at what I want out of life."

"What are you saying, Mum? You've got a lovely life. You're always saying how happy you are working from home. You love the craft fairs and seeing people's faces when they buy your jewellery. What more do you want? I always thought you had everything you ever wanted."

"Good morning, darlings. How are we today? What

a lovely evening we had. Isn't Paul up yet?"

"No, he's snoring away. I think seeing as he's made the effort to come all this way to see me, I'd best take him out and show him the sights and most of all show him I appreciate him coming. You don't mind if we go off by ourselves, do you?"

"Not at all, Amy. Don't hurry back as I'm going to pop over and see Melvin and let him know there'll be one more for dinner tomorrow. I'm sure it won't be a problem and I expect your mum won't mind occupying herself, will you, Heather?"

"Aren't you having any breakfast, Mum?"

"No, I'll get out your way. I'll call at the bakery and pick something up to take up to Edelina's. Have a lovely day and there's no rush to get back. We can all do our own thing this evening as well."

Miriam was in no hurry to go. She made herself a coffee and sat with her book.

"Good morning. Why didn't you wake me? God, look at the sunshine and what a gorgeous view. I can see why you love this place so much, Miriam. It's stunning."

"I know, but promise me that when you go home you don't tell anyone about it. We like to keep it a secret."

"Holkamos – the town of many secrets. That could be a title for a book."

"Paul, it would take many books to tell all the secrets. Now you two have a lovely day. I'm off to read my book."

"Hi, what do you fancy doing today?"

"Well, I thought I'd show you a little bit of the island. We could go to the beach and have some lunch. How does that sound? To start with, on the way down to the beach there's a very special place. It wasn't here when we used to come. It's new and very exciting."

"I'm intrigued and really looking forward to spending the day with you. No phones, no computers, just the two of us."

They got themselves ready and headed for the new

and exciting place. Of course it was the new bakery and Paul agreed it was very special. They filled their bag with pastries and pies. Amy didn't want to get the boat to Volmos because she believed everybody's first sea taxi ride should be coming back into Holkamos harbour at night with all the twinkling lights. It's a sight no one ever forgets, so they sat in the harbour eating their pastries and watching all the little boats coming and going. After eating they walked up the hill to the castle and half way up they poked their heads in the door of Edelina's shop to say a quick hello before continuing up. Amy wanted Paul to see the view looking down towards the harbour from the entrance of the castle. As a child she had spent hours doing this and she could honestly say that there was never a time, either going up or down, when they didn't have a look down. "It's a tradition," she said, and Paul could understand why.

They continued on their walk, going down the other side and passing some of Amy's favourite restaurants. There it was, between the branches of the trees they could see the beautiful beach.

"What a fabulous place to spend your summer holidays. You were so lucky."

"Yes, and as I got older I always knew it was special and appreciated it. Our favourite part of the beach is at the end before you go over the little bridge. See that bit there has the road coming down, but the further along you go it's just sand and a few apartments. It's so quiet. Can you see the colour of the sea?"

They walked down to the edge of the sea and then across to a couple of sunbeds.

"Come on. Let's get in the water before we tan ourselves. It's so warm. It's like getting into a bath." That's how Amy and Paul spent the day, in and out of the sea, lying in the sun completely relaxed. No work, just time together and for the majority of the time Andréas was far from Amy's mind. She was beginning to feel pleased that Paul had arrived.

Miriam phoned Melvin to see what he was doing and ask whether it was alright for Paul to come with them. He was happy to hear her voice and suggested driving over and picking her up to go out for the day. Miriam agreed, saying how nice that would be and that she was in no hurry to get back as both Heather and Amy were spending the day doing their own things.

At the shop Heather and Edelina had enjoyed their pastries and were looking through some websites of clothing suppliers. Edelina wanted to order in one more range for the end of season, something slightly warmer for the cooler September evenings.
"Oh, I forgot to tell you. I've ordered something. I hope you don't mind but I'm having it delivered here; it should be delivered tomorrow."
"I'm intrigued, Heather. Please gives me a clue."
"It's coming from Athens and that's your only clue."
As it was another very hot day the shop was quiet as most people were on the beaches. Heather suggested helping sort out the workshop come storeroom, but Edelina said that was boring and that once the door was closed she didn't see how untidy it was. Heather insisted and said she was sure that if it was clean and tidy she might get the urge to start creating something from all the fabric she had bought all those years ago.
"You're very bossy, Heather. Perhaps you should come over every May as the season starts and help me to get organised."
"Less of the chatter. Before we finish, I want to see this room looking like a professional workroom."

Melvin picked Miriam up and for a change they drove up into the mountains and passed through lots of little villages before stopping at a restaurant overlooking miles and miles of fabulous scenery.

"This is stunning. You'd never guess that we're only a few miles from the sea. It feels as though we're in the wilderness."

They had a lovely lunch and laughed and chatted about the things they had done since they last met. Any talk of what had happened between them had been forgotten for the time being. After a very long lunch they drove back to Volmos, sat in the garden and enjoyed the late afternoon sun. Miriam was having a really nice time and to thank Melvin she insisted on cooking dinner for him which he agreed to. Together they deadheaded the flowers and watered the garden. As the sun moved away from the back, beautiful jasmines made the garden smell as good as it looked. It really was a gorgeous sanctuary.

Amy and Paul had a lovely day on the beach. It was just what they both needed. They stayed there until the sun went behind the mountains. Most of the holiday makers had left the beach as it was the time when the local Greek residents came down for a swim and the beach took on a different life. Umbrellas and sunbeds had been packed away and the sea taxis were coming and going taking people over to Holkamos town for the evening.

"What would you like to do now? We could go back and change and go out to dinner or we could find something to eat before we go back."

"I don't mind. Can you be bothered to go all the way back and then out again? We don't look scruffy. Let's get something on the way back up."

Amy remembered there was a lovely little restaurant in the back streets that only the locals went to. It wasn't anything fancy but they served the most fabulous moussaka. They wouldn't look out of place in their beach clothes and so they walked back up the hill to the castle. Instead of going down past all the shops into the harbour, they took a left turn and twisted and turned among the side streets of houses until they finally arrived at the restaurant. It was busy with a lot of older people. They started with a large plate of tzatziki and warm bread, washed down with a jug of red wine and as for the moussaka, it was just to die for! They were both full and declined the dessert menu. On the way back up to the apartment they stopped to buy a bottle of wine. It was now getting late and they both felt a little tiddly, but happy as they had had such a lovely day.

Back at the apartment one thing led to another and before long they were both in the shower. It was just like when they had first met. They couldn't take their hands off each other. From the shower they ended up making love on the bed. This was love, not hot sweaty sex but real love. Amy was riddled with guilt and when Paul tried to cuddle her she just wanted to get out the bed as fast as possible.

"Come on. Let's sit on the balcony. It's my favourite time of the day looking down into the harbour. It's so magical with the lights flickering onto the water."

Paul poured them both a glass of wine; it was a lovely warm evening and Holkamos looked stunning all lit up. You could just see the sea taxis leaving the harbour taking people back to Volmos.

"I can see why this place is so special and I'm starting to realise why it's not been talked about. I think there was a lot of unfinished business here the last time you visited. Can I ask about the ring or should I say Andréas? He's very nice and I sense you were very close."

"We were very close. We've known each other since, well, I suppose the day we were born. I was only a few months old when I first came here on holiday and for seventeen years we spent the six-week school holiday together playing and having adventures. When we were fourteen things changed. Hormones kicked in and we weren't those two kids playing in the sea, climbing the rocks and messing around in the restaurants. We started to like each other in a very different way and for four years we kissed and cuddled, but that was all."

"So what went wrong? Why did it end?"

"The last summer we were here was the one before Grandad died. It was strange. Come the end of the holiday, Mum went all quiet. It was like she didn't want to be here and so we didn't spend a lot of time with Melvin and Pearle. I don't know why, but Nan just wanted it to be the four of us. Looking back, I did wonder whether she had an inkling about Grandad's death. Did she know in a strange way that the four of us would never come back again? I don't know, but it wasn't the same and up to a few weeks ago I believed Holkamos had run its course. It was the past."

"But now what do you think, Amy? Is it in the past or is Greece the future?"

"For me, the future isn't here. I have a very special life in England with a man I love and want to be with forever but coming back here has opened up old wounds. I did love Andréas and never wanted to see or think about him ever again. He hurt me. Receiving a letter telling me he was seeing someone else hurt, but after a while I got over it and started my adult life."

"But coming back has opened the old wounds. You still wear the same ring as he does. What's that all about? Surely after he hurt you so badly, the last thing you would want is to be reminded of him all the time."

"I don't know why I wear it, I really don't, and it was a shock to see he still wears his. I love you, Paul. You're all I want. We have so much together and after the special day we've had today, I want us to have lots more just like it."

The door opened and in came Miriam. Paul was annoyed as he wanted to ask Amy some more questions.

In his heart he hoped and prayed that Amy coming back here had helped her put everything with Andréas where it belonged – in the past.

Chapter 12

The following morning Amy was up early. Miriam joined her on the balcony where they sat drinking their coffee.

"What have you got planned for today, Nan?"

"Nothing really. I'm looking forward to us going to Melvin's for dinner tonight."

"Why don't we all have a day on the beach together? That would be really nice."

"Oh, no, darling. You and Paul go off together. You don't want me hanging around."

"I do, Nan. If there was ever a day I needed you, it's today. Trust me."

Within minutes Paul was up and Heather was coming out the room all ready to go out. She explained all about the parcel that was being delivered and they were very excited for her. Amy had never seen her mother as happy as she had been these last few days. Although Heather was always a happy and positive person, there was something different about her and Amy thought it was all down to Edelina. Miriam was also pleased to see Heather enjoying her holiday, but she also realised that things were about to change. Life as they had known it since Rex had died was going to be shaken up. Miriam wasn't sure that it was for the better, but had other things to worry about.

"Now you have a nice time, Heather, but remember we're going to Melvin's tonight for dinner. Don't be late back, and as for you two youngsters off to the beach, I've got my volleyball net ready, so I hope you're both up for it. I'm only joking, but I thought we could spend the day on the town beach. We could get some breakfast on the way. I'm off to get ready. Have a lovely day, Heather."

Paul was disappointed. He was hoping that he and Amy could spend the day together alone. He wanted to continue the conversation from last night. He had a feeling there was more to say – they wouldn't get an opportunity to discuss it tonight and tomorrow he would be heading home.

Heather was excited. She hoped the parcel wouldn't arrive before she got to the shop. She rushed to the bakery and found herself running up the hill. By the time she got to the shop, Edelina had put the outside stock out. She had started working early today. They had both had such a lovely time together yesterday and achieved so much tidying up in the workroom, getting rid of empty boxes and finding stock from years ago which she had forgotten about. The shop had taken on a new, fresh look and new stock always brought people in.

"Good morning. You've been busy."

"Well, I thought I'd best get ahead as there's a delivery today. I'm beginning to get excited."

"Who said the parcel would be for you? We'll just have to wait and see. Let's have a coffee and eat our pastries. I need to leave early today as we're off to dinner at Melvin's tonight."

The few days they had spent together had been fun and it was not just Edelina's company that Heather was enjoying. She loved being involved with the shop and she knew that all her ideas had been appreciated. The one thing that hadn't been discussed was the kiss. There had been times when they had been moving stock or passing something to each other that their hands had touched, and it was as if time had stood still for a few seconds. They looked at each other, these were special moments for Heather. Her heart beat faster and her stomach jumped with excitement.

*

Miriam had found three sunbeds by the edge of the water and knew she had planned it perfectly when she saw Amy mouth the words 'thank you'. Miriam had placed herself on the middle bed between Amy and Paul. Paul didn't realise that this had been done on purpose and Miriam continued with this all day. She didn't let them have a single minute to themselves, but she did wonder what had happened. What was Amy's secret? When Paul returned to England tomorrow, she may find out.

Back at the shop, not one but three parcels had arrived. Heather was teasing Edelina by saying that there was no rush to open them. It could wait until later, but secretly she was as excited as Edelina was and just wanted to open the packaging.

"Oh, come on, if you insist. You do it as in an odd way, it is for you."

She opened the first one and to her amazement she could see that it was beads and chains.

"It seemed silly waiting to get back to England to make some jewellery for you to sell and then have to send it over, so I've been online and had just a few bits sent from Athens. I've got just under a week to gets some items made. You'll be able to have some input into this, so come on, open the others. Somewhere in those boxes is a soldering gun. I'm not leaving here today until we make something."

Heather and Edelina were like two children going through all the bits and pieces, putting different colours together and deciding what worked well together and which items would look good with which outfit. It was very exciting and by the end of the day they had put together a plan of action, making four necklaces which they put on display in the shop. Heather had also left a few simple things for Edelina to do if the shop was quiet.

"This is why you were so insistent that we sorted out

the stock room."

"No, not the stockroom, the workroom."

"Thank you so much, Heather. Not just for the jewellery and giving me help with the shop, but I really did need a second opinion on everything from stock to presentation. I suppose I'd got a little bit stale with it all. Most importantly I know we started off on the wrong foot all those years ago but I'm so glad you came back. I'm hoping and praying it won't be another ten years before I see you again."

"No, I can promise you that, it definitely won't be another ten years. I should be the one thanking you as you've opened up my mind and that's something I'll always be grateful for. I don't want go now, but I do have to."

And with that Heather stretched over and gave Edelina a kiss.

"See you tomorrow. The first thing I'll be doing is a quality control check on the jewellery you're going to be producing while I'm not here."

Back at the apartment they were all getting ready and Miriam had continued irritating Paul all day. She was tired and had lost count how many times she'd been in and out of the sea. They had booked a taxi to take them to Melvin's and Miriam was hoping they would eat in the garden because it was so beautiful. Heather was chatting to Amy about the jewellery and what a lovely day she'd had.

"Right, you three. The taxi will be here in a few minutes. Has everyone got everything they need?"

"Nan, you sound like you're getting us organised to go to school."

The short taxi ride was over in no time. This was the first time Heather and Amy would have seen the house for ten years, but it didn't conjure up the same emotion for them as it did for Miriam. They pulled up outside and Melvin was at the gate ready to greet them. After introducing himself to Paul, Melvin led them through to the garden.

"I thought we would eat outside tonight, if that's alright."

"Melvin, the house looks so different. It's so much brighter now. I remember it being full of pine, a pine kitchen, pine furniture, pine door. It looks so much bigger now, don't you think, Amy?"

"Oh yes. Can we come and stay in it as it is now?"

"Of course, Amy, anytime. The house next door is very similar but set more for rental. It's not got all the bits and pieces like this one does and it's not so personal. Come through to the garden."

They were amazed at how it looked. It was completely different and so beautiful. Heather could not get over it, but it wasn't the garden Miriam was looking at. It was the stunning table complete with candles and lights. It was set for ten, five more than she was expecting. Who else was coming?

"Who would like a drink? I think I can cater for all requests."

Paul had a beer and the others wine. Miriam showed them around the garden, smelling the fragrant jasmines. With that two small children appeared, running behind Melvin followed by Carolina and her daughter-in-law. There were more introductions, hugs and kisses. Amy's heart beat fast. Oh, my God, she thought to herself. I had sex with your husband a couple of days ago. How the hell can I act normal? Oh please, I hope Andréas isn't here too. That's the last thing I need.

"Oh, Melvin. This is so lovely. It's just like the old days when we were all here. Carolina, it's so lovely to see you. You've not changed at all, and now you're a grandmother."

"Yes, Miriam. It's so good to have you back on the island. Please don't leave it so long again."

Melvin had served another round of drinks and explained that he was doing a barbeque and hoped that would be alright for everyone. Heather asked Carolina how Andréas was and she said he was hoping to finish work early so he could join them. This was turning into a nightmare for Amy. She knew she had to stick it out and not make an excuse to leave as people might put two and two together. In some respects, it was a good thing the children were there as that helped to break the ice. Andréas' wife, Katia, was very quiet but very sweet and it was obvious that she was a lovely mother.

Miriam insisted on helping Melvin and in a strange way she took control without even Melvin realising it. He got the barbeque going and she brought out the salads and bread and topped up people's drinks. At one point Heather looked at Melvin and then at Miriam and they were smiling at each other. For a brief second she thought it was the same kind of smile that her mum gave Rex when they were having a party. It was real team work.

Then came the moment Amy was dreading. Should she just sit in the corner? No, she realised that she needed to put on an act and be normal. What would have happened in a situation like this if the events of the other afternoon, hadn't occurred?

"I'm sorry I'm late, Melvin. We've been busy and I didn't want to leave them to do everything."

"That's fine, your timing is perfect. Help yourself to a drink as we're nearly ready to eat."

The children were so happy to see their dad and jumped all over him. Katia started to relax more as she wasn't trying to entertain them and stop them from damaging the garden. Paul and Amy were the only ones not enjoying themselves. Amy made more of an effort to make Paul feel welcome, but sensed Andréas felt annoyed. She went and sat next to Katia and began to talk.

"Right then. Everything's ready. There's burgers, sausages, lamb and pork chops. Sit yourselves up to the table and dig in."

"You sit with me, Katia, and I'll will tell you all about that husband of yours when we were children. We got into so much trouble, most of the time for things he did."

Once everyone had started to eat the atmosphere became more relaxed. Paul and Andréas were talking sport and Heather was telling Carolina all about Edelina's shop and the jewellery, and Melvin and Miriam were just so happy to be in each other company, taking it in turn to make drinks and clear plates. It was a real team effort and the evening turned out to be a great success. However, just like Miriam, someone else was taking notes. Carolina had noticed people's faces and reactions. She had put two and two together and from what she had seen it definitely added up to four.

To everyone apart from Miriam and Carolina it was the perfect party. Talking about the old times, what they had all been up to over the last ten years made for a really lovely evening.

"Thank you for all your help tonight, Miriam. I could not have managed without you. What a lovely time we've had. Apart from when my son and grandchildren are here, the house is lonely and sad but tonight it was alive. It was just like the old days. Also, I didn't feel sad that Pearle and Rex weren't here in person. Do you know why? It's because it felt as if they were still part of it. I know that sounds odd and to some people stupid, but I could hear them in my head laughing and joking with us."

"Yes, you're right, Melvin. Thank you for inviting us. I'm beginning to realise that I've missed too many years away from this beautiful Greek island and the special friends I have here."

On the way back in the taxi Paul commented that it

was a lovely way to spend his last night in Holkamos. Amy breathed a sigh of relief. She hoped her acting had paid off.

"I know, it was a lovely evening. Mum, don't you think it was good to be back in the house after all these years? Melvin has made the garden look stunning. Yes, we've had a lovely nostalgic evening, don't you think, Amy? And to think that little boy you played with for all those years now has children of his own. He's so grown up and as for Katia, she's really lovely. They make a great couple."

When Carolina and the family got back home Katia put the children to bed and then went to bed herself. Andréas went to sit in the garden as his head was all over the place. Carolina pottered around for a while to give him some space, but after about 20 minutes she went out to him.

"I've poured us both a drink? Do you want to talk about it?"

"Talk about what, Mum?"

"Okay, Andréas, we can sit here and pretend everything's fine, but you know as well as I do that things aren't."

"I don't know what you're talking about."

"Okay, if you want to play this silly game, I will start. A family arrives back in Holkamos after a ten-year break. One of the family was your girlfriend all that time ago. Since then she has moved on with her life and you now have a wife and two children, but suddenly over the last couple of days I'm guessing you have both remembered the good times you had as teenagers a long time before you became adults with responsibilities. Am I right, Andréas?"

Andréas started to cry and Carolina put her arms around him. They sat there in silence, neither was angry with the other.

"I understand. I really do. Suddenly you've got the

opportunity to have some fun. Since your dad died and your children were born, everything has fallen on you to provide for the family. Now all of a sudden you can go back to being that carefree young man who just loved to have a good time and you're still young. You should be having fun, but sadly that comes with a price."

"How do you know all this?"

"Because I'm your mum and for the last couple of days you've not been yourself. Tonight you joined in just like Amy did. You both put on a show for everyone, but deep down you both wanted to be somewhere else, somewhere quiet and beautiful under the stars. Am I right?"

"Yes, Mum, you're right, and I'm so sorry."

"Sorry for what, Andréas? You're only human. If you weren't upset, there'd be a problem and that would be that you didn't care for your family. One day we think life is all set out for us and we're the happiest we can be, but then something gets thrown at us and we don't know what to do. Do we catch it and run or do we throw it back?"

"You're so wise, Mum. I really wish I could be more like Dad. He wouldn't have looked twice at this. He had you and me. He was a strong man and I can never be as good as him."

"Now, that's where you're wrong, Andréas. Even someone as good as your father can get tempted. Trust me, I know. The thing is, the older you get life doesn't get any easier. In fact, it gets harder. This is something I was never going to tell you, but I think you need to hear it.

"Back when you were three years old your father and I were working day and night through the season. There's nothing unusual about that, but we hardly had any time to spend with you and the little time we did have we were both so tired and irritable. One morning I noticed your dad was acting differently. He was eager to get to the restaurant and seemed to have taken more time getting ready. As he kissed me goodbye, I noticed he'd had taken a clean T-shirt with him and I knew exactly what that meant.

"All the years of working in restaurants taught me that if a waiter came to work with a spare shirt he had a date after work. Now cutting a long story short, yes, he did have several dates with a holiday maker over two weeks and I gave him an ultimatum. Me or her? You see, Andréas, I wasn't going to fight for him. Just suppose I had won, but he wasn't happy. What type of life would we have had? He chose me and you, and there was never a day when he wasn't sorry for what he had done. I believe it never happened again, so I forgave him and never once reminded him about it. He made a mistake. We all make mistakes, but it's how we put things right and move on that counts.

"I would never want you or Katia to be unhappy, but, Andréas, it's something you have to sort out and decide where you want your future to go. I think I've said enough and it's time for bed, but one last thing. Whatever you decide to do, I will always love you and be here for you."

Chapter 13

The following morning the three of them were up early as Paul had to get off to the airport to catch his plane back to England. Again, Miriam purposely kept getting in the way, which Amy was pleased about. They waved him off and then had coffee and pastries. Heather had texted Edelina because she felt she should spend the day with Miriam and Amy. Why she thought this she wasn't really sure but as much as she wanted to get involved with the jewellery making and being with Edelina at the shop, she also wanted to be with her mum and daughter.

"It's still early. Let's make a day of it. What do you both fancy doing? Let's have an adventure."

"Don't you want to be going up to the shop, Mum? Anyway, I don't have an outfit that's suitable for an adventure."

"I don't mean an expedition, just something different. I know, why don't we go over to Corfu? We can catch the boat, take a bag with some overnight things in and come back tomorrow. What do you say to that? It will be fun. All the years we've been coming here, we've seen Corfu in the distance, but never been there."

"This is like a mini gap year, or in our case two days. I've never done something like this in my life."

"Neither have we, Mum. Just a few hours ago we hadn't even planned or thought of this and now here we are eating an omelette in Corfu town. How exciting is this!"

They had a lovely lunch and then a little walk around the town. A cricket match was being played in the centre and the shops were a lot busier. There were far more people here than on Holkamos, but then Corfu was a lot bigger. Their feet were starting to ache, so they stopped for a coffee. Amy got her phone out and started to look for somewhere to stay. Not too far was the holiday resort of Dassia with its sandy beaches and quiet coves and it was only a short taxi ride away. Amy booked a family room for the three of them in a very posh hotel, but as it was only one night she did a deal for less than fifty euros. It was beautiful, just a few metres from the beach.

By the time they had showered and changed, it was getting on for nine o'clock. They weren't in the mood for the hotel restaurant and wanted to find a little restaurant a short walk away. They found one, busy but with a lovely atmosphere, and you could still see the sea.

"This is so lovely and it's nice to go somewhere different, don't you think?"

"Yes, I do, Amy. It's been a lovely little trip. Talking of trips, did I do the wrong thing to bring us back to Greece? Should it have stayed in the past?"

"I think at the time you first mentioned it, Mum and I weren't happy about it, but there have been so many positives. Mum with her jewellery, for example. I've never seen her so excited and it's been lovely to see Melvin and what he's done to the house as well as just being on Volmos. I really had forgotten how special that beach is. How could we have not missed lying on the beach, going in and out the sea? It's Paradise and only a few hours away from England."

"But, Amy, there have been some negatives, hasn't there?"

"Oh yes, Nan. I was hurt. I know I was young, but to get a letter from someone who I was so close to. Okay, we only saw each other for a few weeks every year, but I did love him and to be told he loved someone else was horrible. It took me a long time to get over that."

"But, darling, that was a part of your life that's in the past. You've got Paul now and that's where your future is."

"Your mum's right, Amy. Is your future with Paul?"

"I don't know. I thought so until we came back. I feel things have been opened that were locked away. Good things and bad things. I'm not sure."

"I know exactly what you mean, Amy, and the word you're looking for is 'secrets'. I'm a lot older than both of you and I'm not saying this is right. Most people would say I was definitely wrong, but if a secret is something only you know and no one else and it's not hurting anyone, surely it's okay, don't you think?"

"But sometimes secrets have to come out and be acted on, so perhaps Mum bringing us on holiday is a way to look at those secrets again."

"Come on, we're getting a little bit morbid. We still have nearly a week's holiday and I'm sure by the end of it everything will become clear. Now, you youngsters, what else are we supposed to get up to on these two days away? For a start, I think we should order some more wine."

The subject of secrets did not come up again. The evening was very special for all three of them. Deep down they knew what they had to do and where their lives were going. Would people get hurt along the way? Only time would tell.

Chapter 14

Back on Holkamos after their two days away, Heather was excited to see the progress Edelina had made with the jewellery, and no sooner had they got to the apartment she showered and left to go to the shop. Miriam was tired. It had been a busy couple of days and all she wanted to do was put her feet up. Amy phoned Paul.

"Hi, did you have a good time? It looked like you did from the photos you sent."

"Yes. It was Mum's idea, and we've enjoyed ourselves. We're tired from all the walking and sightseeing, but it was good to get away from here for a bit. Ever since we got to the island we don't seem to have stopped doing our own thing. It was nice to just sit as the three of us and take stock."

"I miss you," Paul told her and added, "I realise that going back there and seeing Andréas wasn't easy for you. Perhaps it's a good thing that you've both grown up and moved on, and that life has changed so much. He has his wife and children now, and you have me and our little business."

"Yes, you're right. I'm looking forward to coming home."

It was nearly seven in the evening. Miriam had fallen asleep and probably wouldn't get up until the morning. Amy was tired but hungry, so she showered and walked down to the harbour. She turned right at the bottom of the hill, in the opposite direction to where Andréas worked. She was just deciding what she fancied: a pizza would be nice or was she more in the mood for moussaka? There came a tap on her shoulder.

"Hello, Amy, how are you? What a lovely evening we

had at Melvin's!"

"Oh hi, Katia! Yes, it was nice, we all enjoyed it. Where are the children?"

"Over there with Carolina. I've just finished work."

"We've just come back from Corfu and I was hungry. I can't make up my mind what I want to eat, though."

"I'm starving. I've not eaten a thing since this morning. If you don't mind, can I join you? I've got time to spare as I'm not meeting Andréas till after ten."

The last thing Amy needed right now was to sit and chat with the wife of someone who she had had sex with: how wrong was that? But she couldn't get out of it. Katia suggested a little pizza and pasta restaurant, and on the way there they chatted about Corfu and the good time they were having.

Once at the restaurant they ordered a pasta dish each and a glass of wine. Amy was feeling so uncomfortable. Katia was nice and she really couldn't dislike her. They were both nearly finished when Katia suddenly became serious.

"This is awkward," she began. "But, you see, things have changed since you've arrived. Andréas is different. He seems distant, like his mind is on something else; and I think the something else is you. It's not your fault, or his, come to that. From what Miriam said, I gather you tried everything not to come back to Greece, so it's not like you've had an urge to see Andréas. He keeps reassuring me that he loves me and that the children are the most important thing in his life. You also have Paul, so from the outside it looks like things have moved on but there's still something bothering me, a little niggle. Amy, I love him and I don't want to lose him. Please tell me it's over and you have no interest in my husband."

"Oh, Katia, it was years ago when we were teenagers. Surely you had crushes on boys when you were fourteen or fifteen? That's all it was. Yes, he hurt me when he told me about you, but it's been ten years since then, and we've grown up. I am happy for him, happy for both of you. I really am."

"Thank you, Amy. That's just what I wanted to hear. I'm sorry for even mentioning it."

Amy thought how awkward it was that they had had their pasta and talked about everything, but she still just wanted to run away. If she could get on a plane and fly back to the UK right now she would, but she knew deep down that would be another secret left behind.

Up at the shop Heather and Edelina were enjoying themselves. The jewellery that she had attempted to make wasn't that good. It really wasn't her thing, but there was no harm done. Heather could take it all apart and start again, but not tonight. It was late, the shop was busy, and they were taking it in turns stopping for something to eat in the workroom. They told each other how much they had missed one another the last few days, but quickly moved on as they knew Heather's holiday would soon be over.

Edelina called into the workroom: "Heather, you have a visitor!"

Amy couldn't face going back to the apartment, so she had walked up to the shop. The three of them chatted for a while and Heather showed Amy all the things she had delivered.

"With all of that, I don't think you will be coming home very soon! It's going to take you months to make all of that up."

"Don't be silly, a couple more days and it will be sorted. Now, I think it's time for us to make a move. We need to bring all the stock in from outside, and then it's nearly time to close up for the day."

"Edelina, are you telling me you do this seven days a week, five months in the year, without a day off, ten in the morning till midnight? You must be exhausted."

"No, Amy. I don't get tired of this, but it would be nice to have the odd day off; I do miss that."

"Why don't you have tomorrow off, and you and Mum can go somewhere nice for the day? I'll run the shop. I can't promise any jewellery will be made, but I'm good at selling."

"No, you're on your holiday, I couldn't let you do that. You and Heather go out for the day."

"Oh, don't say that, Edelina," Heather interrupted. "Amy's offered; take her up on it. We will be back up first thing in the morning. Think of where you want to go on your day off. Yes, a day off, and in August!"

The following morning, Heather and Amy were up at seven as they were determined to be at the shop for half eight. Miriam was also up and thought it was a lovely idea. She even said she might pop up and keep Amy company in the afternoon.

As they were getting themselves ready, Amy noticed a text. It was from Andréas:

"Thank you for reassuring Katia, but can I see you?"

She texted back and told him that she couldn't see him today, as she was running the shop.

"Good morning," Edelina, greeted them. "You're both very early! Are you sure you're alright with this, Amy?"

"Yes! Go and have some fun, I'll be fine here."

Edelina smiled and gave her the keys.

"If it gets too much or you get bored, just lock up and go."

"Go and enjoy yourself. I won't tell you again."

It was a bit early to open the shop, so Amy made a coffee, got stuck in to a pastry, and updated some social media for the other businesses she worked for. She thought that perhaps she could marry the two jobs today. She would obviously have time to Tweet and use Facebook, and the clothes might come in very handy.

At around ten she decided to start setting the shop up. She was looking for the right key in order to start taking the stock out and hang it on the hooks outside, when she noticed someone standing at the door. As she turned the key in the lock, her stomach felt excited. This should not be happening!

"Hello, I had to see you. I can't think of anything else. Can I come in?"

Amy locked the door behind them and led him into the back room. In her head all she wanted to do was to rip Andréas' clothes off and feel his naked body on top of hers, but she knew that this would be wrong. Not just because they would both be cheating, but because this had to stop before it had a chance to begin.

"Amy, let's run away together. Just me and you: we can have a fresh start. Whether we go somewhere else in Greece, or back to England, everything will be okay. Katia and Paul will get over it. All I want is to be with you. I don't care where it is."

"Don't you love your children, and your wife?"

"I do, but I love you more."

"No, you don't," she told him. "You're attracted to me. You want me and God, Andréas, I want you so badly, but it can't happen. You chose Katia over me all those years ago, and there's no turning back. A relationship cannot just be about sex and passion. There must be more, something that will stay far longer than any passion. This is where it ends. I'm so sorry. If you want to give up on your family, that's your business but I'm not going to be part of it.

"Andréas, what happened the other day shouldn't have. It was wrong. I'm not saying I didn't enjoy it, because it was far better than anything I could ever have dreamt of, but that was it. As much as I may want it again, it's not going to happen. I'm sorry, but this really is where it ends."

She picked the keys back up and headed out into the shop. He followed, not saying a word. He didn't even look at her as she unlocked the door. Then he was gone. She felt sick but she knew, even though it wasn't the thing she wanted to do, it was the right thing to have done.

Andrea walked back to his bike. He sat there for a few minutes, wondering how Amy's feelings could change like that in just a couple of days. They could make a go of it, he was sure, and it was not just about the passion. She had admitted that what he had with her was good. I'm not giving up, he decided. I can bring her around. I know I can!

Edelina had decided to take her car and get away from the town for the day. There were so many lovely coves that only the locals knew about, but before they could have a day on the beach she wanted a breakfast. She knew just the place.

About three miles from Holkamos town, down a little lane, was a café with only five tables inside and about the same number outside. The man who owned it had been there for years and cooked the best omelettes you've ever tasted. So much so, that after many years of offering other types of food as well, he had ended up just serving omelettes and nothing else.

"I've never tasted anything like it!" said Heather. "And, Edelina, just look how busy he is. What a lovely life he has."

"The eggs he made the omelette from were probably only laid in the last few hours. He has his own chickens out the back in a little field. I'm sure it's because they're so happy and well looked after that they lay such beautiful eggs."

After breakfast they headed a few more miles along the coast until they got to another little track, which was incredibly bumpy and seemed to go on for miles, but eventually led to a little cove. There were a few cars parked there, but the beach was so out of the way that it was almost private.

"Heather, can you help me carry a few things I've got

in the boot of the car?"

"I didn't see you put anything in the car apart from our beach bags," said Heather, confused.

She opened the boot, only to find a huge umbrella and a picnic basket in there! Edelina explained that she had been up early and been to the bakery. Heather thanked her for the lovely surprise, and they climbed down a little bank and across some rocks to set up camp for the day. All you could hear was the sea slowly and calmly moving in and out. It was Paradise.

"This is so lovely," Edelina sighed. "I can't thank Amy enough for holding the fort. She's a lovely girl, you must be so proud of her."

"I am. She's never given me a day's trouble. When other people go on about their kids being so disobedient or in trouble for doing the wrong thing, it does make me think. But I've my mum and dad to thank as well. She might not have had her own father in her life, but she has had three parents."

The whole day was spent going in and out of the sea and chatting about each other's past. Every now and again their hands touched and one or the other would lean over to kiss the other one. Everything felt so natural and normal for both of them. The one thing that wasn't talked about was the future, but today wasn't the time for it. Today was a special day, and deep down they both knew that they didn't want it to be the only one. Both Heather and Edelina wanted to have lots of special days together.

"Hello, darling, how are you doing? I hope it's not too boring for you."

"Hi, Nan, the time's flown by, actually. When I've not had any customers, I've been working on the Internet. Let me get you a chair and we can sit and chat. I don't think there will be many people coming in. It's too nice a day; they will all be on the beach."

Amy made them both a coffee, and they talked about the holiday, the things they had done, how lovely Melvin was, and the house.

"So, Amy, what happens when you get home? Do you and Paul have things to sort out? Will everything be as it was before you came away, or have things changed?"

"If you'd asked me that a few hours ago, I'd have said that things do need to be sorted out, but not now, Nan. When I get home, everything will be back to normal, I promise you."

"That's what you think, but will Paul think the same?"

"I reckon once he sees I've taken this stupid ring off he'll know exactly how things are. Talking of the ring, I think it's time it came off and went in the bin. It's a symbol of a past without any future. Perhaps it had some hope, but not anymore."

"Darling, don't put in in the bin! Let me look after it for you. That's not me saying it should or could have a future, I'm just saying that it's a memory, and memories are very important. It might be a secret memory, but if it's a secret that didn't hurt anybody, who's to say if it's right or wrong?"

"Thank you, Nan. I'm glad you brought us back to Greece. Sometimes life seems very straightforward, but I think there are times when we need to stop and think and tidy a few things up in our minds. That sounds stupid. I know you probably don't understand what I mean."

"Oh, my darling, I do understand. Those things can be floating around in your head for years. They may go to the back of the mind, but eventually they do need facing up to and putting right. Once that's done you can move on and look to the future."

Miriam and Amy spent the rest of the day mixing and matching clothes, each trying things on, showing off their outfits, and talking to customers. They had a lovely time, and also sold some stock!

Around seven o'clock Edelina asked if they should see whether Miriam and Amy wanted to join the two of them for something to eat back in Holkamos. Heather phoned Amy, who asked about the shop?

"Close it!" Edelina shouted in the background. "Let's have a night out."

"This is so beautiful. How could anyone ever get bored of that view?" Miriam said, as they sat looking out over Volmos. This was a favourite restaurant of hers; she had known the family that owned it for years. The food and wine here were the perfect end to a lovely day as all four of them sat there, each wrapped in their own thoughts.

Miriam was happy that Amy had sorted out her issues with Paul: she was guessing it had something to do with Andréas. Then there was Heather, her loving daughter, who seemed to be starting a new life for herself. She was so happy for her. There might be a few more bridges to cross, but the big steps had already been taken. Now would come the exciting part.

Amy sat there knowing that she had done the right thing. Perhaps not the thing she had wanted to do, but life was not all about having everything you wanted. She knew that her life with Paul was good. She just needed to reassure him that it was.

Heather and Edelina were simply relaxed in each other's company. Deep down they both knew what the future had in store for them. It just needed sorting out.

Miriam took a minute as she came back from the toilet. Was her head sorted? Looking out over the empty beach with its twinkling lights coming from restaurants and apartments she decided that yes, it was, although somehow, she didn't think that was the end of it. Now she needed to look at her heart: something she never thought she would be doing here on Holkamos.

"Come on, you three," said Edelina, "the night is still

young. I know of a little bar half way down the hill where they make the most beautiful hot chocolates. It will be the perfect end to such a special day."

"That would be lovely, Edelina," Amy agreed. "Also: I don't want to interfere but being in the shop today has given me some ideas for necklaces and bracelets. Mum could make the orange beads in different sizes look so good against the white tops. And if it's alright with you, Edelina, I know you've never done it before, but I would like to open an Instagram account for the shop. I'm sure it would bring in some business.

"Also, if you don't mind me saying so, I think you should try and stock some more sandals. They don't really go out of fashion that quickly and holiday makers never bring enough footwear."

Edelina laughed. "In less than two weeks, a family of three women have come to Greece and taken over my shop! A shop that's not really changed much in twelve years."

"Oh, I'm sorry, Edelina! That's not what we intended to do. Please forgive us."

"Forgive you? Don't be so silly, it's the best thing that's ever happened to the shop. Or maybe I should put it a different way: it's the most wonderful and exciting thing that has ever happened to me! Meeting all of you has been so special. Now, before I cry, let's go off for that hot chocolate."

Chapter 15

With just a few days left of the holiday, Heather and Amy were up early. They were both going up to see Edelina, and Amy was going to give Heather a hand at making some necklaces. It would also give her the opportunity to get to know Edelina a little better. Miriam had already made plans to spend the day with Melvin: he was going to pick her up to go out somewhere, but she had texted him to say that she would meet him at his house instead. She was in the mood for a little walk and she loved the short trip on the sea taxi so much. Melvin was pleased, as he wasn't really in the mood to go out. He was at his happiest pottering around his garden.

"It's like a production line going on with you two. I must say, it looks very professional and organised."
"Oh, Edelina, don't stop her. By the time we leave, Mum will have turned your shop from selling clothes to jewellery. You'll have enough items to see you though this summer and the next one."
"Less of the talking, Amy, I'm on a mission to get these done by lunch time. It was your idea about the orange ones: I suggest you get a move on!"

Miriam stopped down in the harbour before getting the sea taxi. She wanted to just sit with a coffee and watch the world go by. Young, old, Greek, Italian, English, German, Swiss: they were all here together in one little town, enjoying the summer sunshine. She felt extremely lucky and blessed to be a part of it. Holkamos was a million miles away from her life in England.
"Hello, Miriam, all by yourself today?"

"Oh hello, Andréas. Yes, Amy and Heather have gone up to Edelina's and started to turn her little shop into a jewellery factory. Have you got time to stop for a coffee before starting work?"

"Yes, that would be nice. I've still got some time before I start work."

"We've messed your life up coming back here and I'm so sorry, Andréas, I truly am, but the thing is that all three of us had to come back. We all had our different reasons, perhaps not all good reasons, but the older you get the more you realise that life is not as straightforward as you think."

"Miriam, I love Amy. I really do. I let her down once, and I can't do it again! I want us to be together for ever."

"Andréas, I'm not in any position to give you advice, and in life we all have our own choices to make, but you just said 'I' five times in a very short period. I really think you should ask yourself what Amy wants and not just what you want. Perhaps the word you should be thinking about is 'we'."

Melvin was pottering in his garden deadheading the cosmos. They were such a bright, cheery flower, and when there was a breeze it looked like they were dancing. He made himself a cup of tea. Strangely, this was one of the times when he would miss Pearle the most. It wasn't so nice just making the one cup. He missed her companionship so much: just having her there when a thought came to mind, to be able to speak it out and listen for a reply. You don't realise how important conversation is until it's gone.

Heather had made five different necklaces. They all looked like they belonged in the same collection, but the colours were different. She was pleased with the way the beads flowed into each other: shades of blue on one necklace, and dark reds on another.

"Right, Amy. Let's see your orange collection. Then you can copy these: I would like to see another five of each, please!"

The three of them laughed together. Heather was so happy that Amy and Edelina were getting on so well together. She knew that in years to come today would be a very special memory for her.

Miriam said her goodbyes to Andréas. He looked a broken man, but he was a man with a family and responsibilities. Just like her, he had to come to terms with life's ups and downs. And now it was time for her to see what life might have in store for her.

The sea taxi pulled up to the jetty on Volmos and as Miriam got off the boat a huge cloud covered the sun. She caught sight of people putting on T-shirts and others wrapping themselves up in their towels. Oh, how she loved this beach. The fun times spent here as a family, even sheltering under the umbrella when it had rained, had given her so many fond memories. She was so deep in her thoughts that she walked in the wrong direction, and before long the little church was in front of her.

A mother cat was sitting with her three kittens in the doorway. As she walked by them into the church, Miriam felt completely different than she had the last time. There was no guilt or wanting to be forgiven now. Rex was in her thoughts: all the happy times here in Greece, but not just that, all of their wonderful years together. She realised she could never love anyone as much as she had loved him. She opened her bag, took out a few euros, placed them in the jar, and lit a candle. Placing it in the little tray of sand next to just one other, Miriam stepped back and stared at the two candles burning away so gently. She felt someone come in behind her. She turned to see who it was, and there was Melvin.

"I hope you don't mind me being here. I can leave if you like, but I was waiting for you to get off the boat and you came this way instead, so I followed."

"Yes, I don't know why I did. I was here before I knew it, but I'm glad I came. There is something so special about this church."

"I know what you mean. I come here a lot, not to be morbid or sad, but to celebrate my life with Pearle. I really don't think it's something I would do in the UK, but here on Holkamos it just seems the right thing to do."

"That's exactly how I feel. This might sound strange, Melvin, but I feel my life was in three parts. The first part was being young and free, exploring life. Then part two was getting married, being a mum, and becoming a grandmother. Now I feel part three is starting for me. This is the final part. I don't want that to sound depressing, but it's true. I'm heading towards the end of my life, hoping and praying it's a long way off, but I think it's time to relax and enjoy my part three."

"I've never looked at it like that, but you're completely right. When people talk about being on a journey I cringe and get slightly annoyed, but in this case we're on a journey, and we're both on the final leg."

"Come on. Let's go back. Oh, sorry, did you want to light a candle, Melvin?"

"I've already done it. That's mine, the one next to yours."

As they turned and walked back out of the little church all of a sudden the big cloud passed away from the sun and there it was, shining as bright as ever: another perfect day in Paradise.

Carolina had a day off from looking after her grandchildren. They were spending the day with some friends, so she decided to walk to Holkamos. On the way she was hoping to call in on Melvin and thank him for the lovely evening. She loved the walk down from Creakos; it was steep, but the views were stunning. She wasn't in a hurry, and the peace and quiet gave her time to think.

She was worried about Andréas and Katia. They were both young and she hoped he would see sense; but more than that she wanted him to be happy. She reached into her bag for her bottle of water. There was a chopped-down olive tree on the bend. She sat on it, and looked out over the olive fields to Volmos in the distance. This was a view she had lived with all her life, and the older she got the more important it became. There was a time when her life could have gone in a different direction, but this was something she didn't want to think about.

Back in Melvin's garden he moved two sun loungers into the shade and poured them both a glass of wine. It felt so comfortable just to have someone to chat with. That's what he missed: companionship.

"You've worked so hard on your garden, Melvin. So much thought has gone into it. I look out and think: oh, that bit there is my favourite, and then five minutes later I think: oh no, I love that bit the most! And although you've broken the garden up into separate areas it all flows and goes together so well, you should be so proud."

"I am, but this last week I've looked at the garden in a different way, because I've been able to talk about it with you. Over the last few years I've just gardened and sat and admired it, but to be able to discuss why I did things, and the reasons I put a plant in a specific place, has made such a difference. It would have been good to be able to talk over whether this or that place was right for a certain plant when I was starting out."

"I think you did very well by yourself. There is nothing I would change."

*

Carolina had been sitting on the log for ages. Her head was all over the place, not just regarding Katia and Andréas, but also occupied with her own mistakes. One of them, anyway: she had put it to the back of her mind years before, but it had happened over twenty years ago. It was so silly, and should never have happened in the first place, but it did. She had been so hurt by her husband's affair. Even if his relationship had only lasted for a couple of weeks, it had still devastated her, but what she had done was just as bad.

One morning she had just taken some clean bedding and towels out to the holiday homes. Everyone had gone to the beach, so first she went and changed the beds in the home Melvin and his family were staying in, and then went next door to where Miriam and her family were. She had knocked on the door just in case someone was there, and Rex answered. He hadn't gone with the others as he had work to do. He had offered to make them both a cup of coffee, which was nothing unusual. They sat and chatted as they had done frequently over the years, and then he offered to carry the big bag of clean linen up the stairs for her. Carolina followed him up.

After he had placed the bag on the bed, as he was making his way back downstairs, they brushed by each other in the doorway. They both stood there for a second and looked at each other. To this day she didn't know what had come over them, but they kissed. Not a peck on the cheek, but a long, slow, passionate kiss, which went on for ages. But that was all. Nothing else happened. It could have, even though he was so much older than her, but they both knew it was wrong. He had made an excuse to leave, and Carolina got her jobs done.

Over the years there were many opportunities for them to be alone together, but they never were. Why and how it had happened she would never know, and it was never talked about. Was it the same situation with Andréas and Amy? She hoped that it would get sorted out before Amy went home to England.

"What's that you've got there, Edelina?"

"It's the euros for the three bracelets and the necklace I've just sold to a lovely German lady. I can't believe two hours ago they weren't even made! I'm going to lock the door on you pair and keep you as slaves, just producing jewellery."

They all laughed. It wasn't just seeing her mum happy with Edelina, but spending time with both of them that felt so good for Amy. But what would happen when they had to go home? What did the future hold for her mum?

Carolina arrived at Melvin's. It was nice that Miriam was there. They chatted about everything, apart from the one thing they needed to discuss, and just like Miriam, she was amazed by what he had done with the garden.

"How about I get us something to eat, what do you say, ladies?"

"I think that would be a lovely idea. While you're doing that, Carolina and I can have a little chat."

"Oh, Miriam. What are we going to do? Andréas is so obsessed with Amy, and what's going to happen if it turns out she feels the same?"

"I really don't think we have anything to worry about in Amy's case. I think her head will overrule her heart. He hurt her once, and I don't think she will let it happen again."

"But what happens if he can't get her out of his mind? Since Amy's been here he's been such a different boy. All the laughter has gone, and he's so fed up with everything."

They sat in silence until Melvin came back with a platter of sandwiches. For the first time, Miriam said to herself that she should never have come back to the island of Holkamos; all the more so because she knew both Heather and Amy had been adamant that they didn't want to. The secrets that the three of them had left here should have been left alone and not revisited. This holiday was going to end with more secrets than it started out with. Why had she opened this can of worms?

Chapter 16

It was the last full day of the holiday. Tomorrow afternoon they would catch the plane back to England. All three of them were up early. Amy had been to the bakery, and they sat on the balcony drinking coffee and eating their pastries. Today felt different: Heather and Miriam felt tense, and there wasn't much conversation. None of them had decided what they were going to do today.

"Are we having a day on the beach? It's not a problem if you don't want to, or if you want to go up to Edelina's shop, I'm easy. How about you, Nan, what do you fancy?"

"I'm happy to go along with what you both want to do."

This went on for what seemed like ages, with no one making a decision until Miriam finally spoke up.

"Right then, I believe this holiday – coming back here to Holkamos – has turned out to be very important for all three of us. As for whether it was the right thing, I'm having my doubts. I somehow think we don't look at things the way we did when we first arrived, but the most important thing is that we don't leave here with our loose ends not sorted out. So why don't we go and do what we all have to, meet back here tonight, and then go out and have a lovely meal to finish off the holiday?"

Amy was first out of the door: she needed to talk to Andréas before he started work. She very much didn't want him to be pining after her after she had gone. He had a good life and a very special family; all they would ever have had together was passion.

Heather was the next to get ready. She was going to walk up and see Edelina. There was no jewellery to make today, as the shop was awash with it even though so much had already been sold, which was exciting for both of them.

Miriam sat on the balcony until they had both gone. Neither Amy nor Heather had really needed anything from her for many years, but up until now she had felt she had to be there for them. This holiday had shown her that times were changing. Things were moving on, and it was time to change. They would still be there for each other but now perhaps a little less. She didn't know if she had done right by insisting they come back to the island, but she could tell that most of the 't's were crossed and the 'i's dotted. It was nearly time to go home, and as for the secrets: had they created even more?

Amy caught sight of Andréas parking his scooter and ran a little to catch up with him. He smiled at her, and she looked into those gorgeous brown eyes: oh, they were to die for!

"Hi, have you got a minute before you start work? I want to say something. Let's walk down to the sea wall."

They walked down together and sat on a bench looking out towards the little island.

"You know in your heart it would never have worked. I'm not saying what happened wasn't good, because my God, it was beautiful. But the passion wouldn't last for ever. What you've got in your life is so very special. A wife and two gorgeous children, that is far more than we could ever have."

"I know you're right, but I just—"

"No, Andréas, stop there. You've said enough; you know I'm right. I want us to be friends, but that has to be as far as it goes, please believe me. Get me out of your head, and your life will be so much better, I promise you. I somehow think I will be coming back here to Holkamos a lot, and we don't need anything to happen between us again. It wouldn't be good for us and, not for our families either."

Miriam decided to go for a walk. She thought she might wander up to the shop, see Heather and Edelina, take another look at the jewellery, and then go to see Melvin. It would be nice to walk to Volmos for a change.

Amy said her goodbyes to Andréas and was intending to spend the rest of the day on the beach: a final top-up of the tan. But as she turned the corner she bumped into Katia.
 "Hi, Katia, not working today? Have you got time for a coffee?"
 "No, I'm sorry, I'm working. I've just had to pop down here from work. If you see Carolina or Andréas, please don't tell them you've seen me! Thank you, Amy, goodbye."
 Katia seemed in a hurry, Amy thought. Also, what was all that about? Why didn't she want to be spotted? It was all very strange.

"Hello, Mum, this is a nice surprise! I thought you might have gone over to see Melvin today."
 "Yes, I'm on my way. I thought I would stop by and see you and Edelina first."
 "Oh, she's gone to see a supplier in Preveza as I'm here to cover the shop. Would you like a coffee? I'm having one. Come through to the workroom."
 "Gosh, this is a big room. It must be the same size as the shop, and so light! Perfect for working in, and you can see people from here if they come into the shop."
 Heather made the coffee and pulled another stool round so they could both sit down.
 "You know, darling, I don't think I've ever seen you so happy. No, sorry, that doesn't sound right. You are always happy, but perhaps I should say content instead.

Are you glad we've come back to Holkamos? I am. It is a very special place.

"Can I say something? I know you worry about me as I'm getting older, but you don't need to. If I need some help at any time I will ask, and as things are at the present time I'm fit and healthy. Also, perhaps it's not my place to say this but... you've been a wonderful mother to Amy and we're both so proud of her, but she doesn't need us like she used to. So I think perhaps it's time to care for yourself: time to have fun and really enjoy life to the full. With your job, it's all done on the computer; you work from home and really, home could be anywhere you choose. As for your jewellery making, all you need is a work space. It's not for me to tell you what to do, but if you moved in here with Edelina I wouldn't have a problem with it. I would actually be very happy for you."

"Oh, Mum, thank you! I'm very happy spending time with Edelina, and I know she's happy with me. We've not talked about the future. To be honest, we haven't talked about anything. I think we are both a little scared to."

"Scared is fine. If anything it's good. It's not for me to tell you what to do, but what I will say is: you have my blessing. I love you very much, and I am so proud of everything you've ever done."

They hugged each other. Both were upset, but happy as well. The shop was starting to get busy. One customer came in and was so excited about Heather's jewellery that she bought a necklace and two bracelets.

"If ever there was a sign that you could have a life here in Holkamos, darling, that was it."

With that, Miriam left. She was very happy for Heather, whatever she decided to do. As she got to the top of the hill she did what they had always done: stand at the entrance to the castle and look down over the harbour. A young woman looked at her and said, "Isn't it beautiful?"

"I know. To me it's more than beautiful. It's a very special place."

Miriam made her way down the steep hill to Volmos. The sea was calm, a few yachts were coming and going, and the beach was busy; it was another beautiful day in Paradise. As she strolled past the little taverns she wondered if she could cope with this twenty-four-seven and not get bored with it. Could you have too much sunshine?

After another half an hour she arrived at Melvin's. It was time for both of them to put their cards on the table, although for her part all the not sleeping and worrying had gone completely. This was now, and not all those years ago.

"Good morning, I've let myself in. You're not still deadheading those cosmos?"

"The more you cut the dead ones off, the more they will flower. It's nice to see you, Miriam. I'll make us a cup of coffee."

"No, you carry on. I'll go and do it."

Andréas' mobile rang. It was Katia, asking if he could pop home for ten minutes sometime during the day. She needed to speak with him, and couldn't do it over the phone. He agreed to come after the lunch period was over. Had she found out about Amy? Oh God, he just wanted to run away!

"Coffee's up! Where are we sitting? If it's alright with you, Melvin, as it's my last day, could it be in the sun and not the shade?"

"It doesn't have to be your last day. You could stay."

"Is that an invitation?"

"Of course it's an invitation. There's nothing I would love more than to spend more time with you. I think there's something I need to say before you leave, but I don't know how to say it without it coming out wrong."

"That's strange, Melvin, because I have something to tell you and I really don't know how to word it either, so who's going to go first? I will. The thing is, what happened all those years ago between us was lovely, but it's not really something that could happen again. We're both older – actually, we are old – and that part of a relationship doesn't interest me anymore. As much as I love your company, I don't think sex will ever happen again between us, and the last thing I want to do is to give you the impression that it will."

"Oh, darling Miriam, how similar we are. That's exactly what's been worrying me! I want to spend time with you as we have so much fun, and I haven't felt this good since before Pearle died, but the whole business of love-making couldn't be further from my mind. I'm so relieved that you feel the same."

They both sat there laughing away to each other, both feeling that they had found a starting point for their relationship to grow.

"So, Miriam, with that out of the way, where do we go from here? The invitation for you to stay here is open; you could have your own room."

"We would be companions for each other, Melvin. Or does that sound too formal?"

"Yes, far too formal. We would be two very dear friends spending the last years of their life together, having fun, and keeping each other young. Friendship: how can anything be better that that?"

As Andréas closed the door and took one last look at Katia looking out of the window, he was still in shock. This wasn't meant to happen. His head was ready to explode, but he knew he had to get back to work. It was August, and Holkamos was the busiest it had been all season. All he kept thinking of as he drove back down from Creakos was what his mother would say. Then he thought about the other day, making love to Amy. It had been like being 17 again. Young, free, single, no responsibilities, but was that really the way he wanted to live his life? He knew that wasn't the right way. Come on, Andréas, he told himself, pull yourself together.

Edelina came back from Preveza with a few bits of stock, but she was very quiet and subdued. Heather was feeling the same way. After nearly two weeks of fun together, it was almost time to say goodbye. Neither one knew where they stood with the other. The last thing Edelina wanted to do was upset Heather like she had all those years ago. Over the course of the week they had talked about everything apart from the most important thing: their future. But deep down, both wanted the same thing, and that was each other. The silence was broken by the ringing of Heathers phone.

"Oh hello, Carolina. No, we've not really made any plans. I will phone them and see what they think. Can I call you back in a bit? Okay, bye for now."

"Anything wrong, Heather?"

"No, not really. It was Carolina wanting to know what we are doing with our last evening on the island and wondering if we wanted to go up to her house and eat with her and the family. You are invited as well. It's not what I really fancy doing, but how can we say no?"

It took Heather about half an hour to chat to Amy and Miriam about it, but as they both agreed, Carolina would be upset if they didn't go. She phoned her back and it was all arranged. Edelina and Melvin were going to go as well, so that cheered Heather up.

"You'll be glad when I've gone, at least the shop will be open more! Thanks to me it's been closed for so many evenings."

"Do you know, Heather, if I could keep you in my life, I'd close the shop down. I really mean that. Please tell me that tomorrow isn't goodbye for ever."

"So, on a practical level, how would you eat and pay the bills if you closed?"

"Don't be practical, Heather. It's been the best couple of weeks of my life, and I want it to continue."

"And so do I, but we need to give it some thought. I can reassure you of one thing: tomorrow is not goodbye forever. Now I need to get back to the apartment and get ready for the evening, so I will see you later."

Back at the apartment, the three of them kept themselves busy with packing and sorting out their outfits for the evening. Miriam was slightly worried about Amy, but there was no need to be. In her head, she had sorted everything out with Andréas in the morning, and she was looking forward to getting back to Paul. The holiday had been fun, and now it was time to move on. Two taxis had been booked. Edelina was going to share one with Melvin; he was going to walk up from Volmos and meet her near the castle.

Andréas had a chat with his uncle, and he agreed that he could leave work at eight, which was not really the answer he had wanted. Something told him that this evening with everyone all together was not a good idea, but as Carolina had texted him so many times telling him not to be late how could he upset his mother by not being there?

When they arrived, Carolina and Katia were busy in the kitchen. The children were playing in the garden. It was a lovely August evening, but up here in Creakos it was a lot cooler than down in Holkamos, and there was a lovely cool breeze.

"Come in, come in. It's so lovely to have you all here on your last night! Go through to the garden and I'll get us a drink. Andréas has promised me he'll be here shortly; his uncle is letting him finish work early but then, seeing that he is my brother, he didn't have much choice. He daren't upset his big sister."

Melvin was looking around the garden. Oh, how he

would love to get his hands on it and create something special. From one side you could look right down to Volmos and see the sea, it was such a fabulous view. Amy was chatting to Edelina about the shop and the new stock she had bought today. Miriam helped to carry the glasses of wine out into the garden and was feeling that this would be a lovely end to the holiday. As she went back in to the house she could see that Andréas had arrived, and Carolina was giving him a hug. She didn't want to stare and be in the way, but to her it looked like they were both upset. Katia hadn't noticed, as she was in the kitchen pouring herself an orange juice.

"Daddy's home! Come on, Daddy, come and play with us before we eat!"

"Slow down, you two! I need to go and change and have a drink first."

"What is my companion thinking? To me, it looks like she's miles away."

"Less of this 'companion' business, Melvin. I'm sitting here trying to put two and two together, and it keeps adding up to five."

"Would you all like to sit at the table? The meal's nearly ready. Come on, Melvin, stop trying to plan out my garden. I've told you before, once the grandchildren have grown up I will have lovely flowers, but for now it's more of a football pitch. Right, that's it. Children calm down, where's your dad? Come on, Andréas, Katia, you two sit here, and before we start eating, have either of you got anything to say?"

It suddenly went quiet. Amy was wondering what was coming. Miriam looked at Melvin.

"I've done it. I know. I have made two and two come to four."

"Come on, Andréas, tell them! If you don't, I will. I've never known you to be so shy."

Amy could see that he was looking everywhere apart

from at her. She tried to make eye contact, but he was having none of it.

"Thank you so much for coming tonight. It's been so great to see you all again after all these years. Katia and myself would like you all to be the first to know our news. We're having another baby."

There were cheers and congratulations all around. Everyone was so excited for them, especially Amy, as she knew that this was how it should be. She was so happy that she had come back to Holkamos. She hadn't wanted to in a million years, but even though she would be leaving a big secret behind her, it was a secret both her and Andréas needed to create so that they could both move forward with their lives.

Chapter 17

"Good morning, darling, you're up early after such a very late night. Didn't we have a lovely time? I can't remember when I laughed so much, and I know another thing: once I'm home I'm back on my diet! I've eaten so much, and as for the wine, I think my insides have been pickled."

"Morning, Nan. Yes, it was a lovely evening, and what wonderful news about the baby! I'm so pleased for them. I'm up early as Paul's sent me a message. It's ever so exciting; he just finished creating a website for a jewellery company with about twelve shops, and they're really over the moon with it. They've been around for years and were getting quite old fashioned, but he pulled them into the twenty-first century. Well, the exciting bit for me is that I'm going to be their online manager! They will photograph the jewellery, I will run the Twitter, Facebook, and Instagram parts for them, and Paul will manage their website. It's the first time we've been able to combine both of our businesses together, and hopefully it will lead to more work."

"How lovely, darling. I'm so pleased for both of you. Are you looking forward to going home to Paul?"

"I am, yes. I really am, and, Nan, thank you for bringing me back to Holkamos. I really didn't want to come, and perhaps some secrets still exist on this island for me, but – oh, listen to me, going on like this! Secrets are only bad if someone gets hurt, don't you think?!"

"Amy darling, you've hit the nail on the head. Everything happens for a reason, and as long as no one is harmed along the way, I think secrets are okay. By the way, your mum's late getting up."

"Oh, Mum's been up for hours. She's gone up to see

Edelina."

Heather stood in the bakery, waiting to be served. There were so many things she would miss when she went home, and the pastries, cakes, and bread from here would be near the top of the list. She would miss the weather, too, and the stunning scenery, but the one thing she would miss the most was Edelina. It was not going to be easy to say goodbye today.

It was still early, and as she walked up the hill she could see that Edelina wasn't up yet, as her balcony doors were still closed. Heather decided to go and have one last look out over the harbour. She sat on the wall at the entrance to the castle. It was such a special view. Although her favourite time to look down into the harbour was at night with all the lights flickering in the water, there was something special about this time of day, when the town was waking up: excited holiday makers off to the beach, locals off to get their food shopping done before it got too hot and busy. If she was brave enough, this could be home.

"Good morning, you're late getting up. I thought I'd have to leave a note saying goodbye."

"Come on in. I think it's because I drank a lot last night. I think we all drank too much, but what a lovely evening we had. So, today's the day my shop assistant leaves and I go back to having to fend for myself. How long do you think I have before the clean and tidy workroom becomes a messy store room again?"

"Well, that depends on whether you need a full-time shop assistant, and not just a holiday relief. The assistant might need a little desk in the corner to do her accountancy work, mind you."

They both stood staring at each other. Tears started running down their cheeks. Heather walked towards Edelina and wrapped her arms around her. It seemed to be forever before either of them spoke, but eventually

Edelina pulled away. Still holding on to Heather's hands, she mumbled though the tears, "I've wanted to ask you to stay since the day you first walked in here with your mum and Amy, and every day since, but I've been scared because of what happened last time. I didn't want to frighten you off and never see you again."

"No scaring me off, I'm here to stay! I've never felt so good about anything ever in my whole life. First of all, I've got to go back to England and sort the house out. While I'm doing that, you've the rest of the summer to sell all the jewellery I've made, because there are boxes and boxes more coming back with me."

As the seat belt signs were turned off, the air hostess came along with the drinks trolley. Miriam ordered three little bottles of champagne and made a toast.

"To the three of us. To the past and the future, goodbyes and hellos, but most of all to those secrets that aren't always bad, secrets that lead us to new beginnings and to happiness."

Chapter 18

FIVE YEARS LATER

"Paul, can you bring Rex in? Amy says it's time to get ready for the party."

"We're on our way, Miriam, aren't we, little birthday boy? Or should Daddy say big birthday boy, now you are four?"

Miriam was standing at the patio doors watching them. It was just like the old days when they were here on holiday and she was calling Heather and Amy in. It seemed just like yesterday how all their lives had changed.

"Are you okay, Nan? You look like you're miles away in deep thought."

"I am, darling. It's so lovely that you've come over again for the summer holidays. Yesterday Melvin and I were only saying that it's just like the old days, but now there's a new generation."

"I realise the childhood I spent here on Holkamos was very special and that's just what I want for Rex too. When you first said you were going to spend most of the year here with Melvin my heart sank and then when Mum said she would be here for ever I remember thinking how lost I would feel. But where has the last five years gone? So much has happened with Paul and me moving out of that pokey flat and into Mum's house, our businesses taking off so well and the arrival of Rex. Plus we manage to come here twice a year, but most of all it's so lovely to see Mum so happy. Do you know what I like best about Mum and Edelina's relationship? Their work takes second place. They really enjoy life. The shop and the bookkeeping are just something in the background and as for you, Nan, I always knew no one could take the place of Granddad, but the way you and Melvin tick along is so lovely. I'm so pleased you have each other."

"Thank you, darling. Yes, your mum is so happy. I can see it in both of them all the time, but then it's also lovely seeing you so happy. There was a time when I thought Paul might be out of the picture, but I'm glad he isn't as he's such a good husband and father."

"Yes, I know it was a good job I listened to my head and not my heart. Things could have turned out so different otherwise. I have no regrets, Nan. None whatsoever."

"Yes, Amy. I know what you mean. Many years ago there was a time when my heart could have changed everything for me, but thankfully heart and head came together and made the right choice."

"Come on, you two, less of the chit chat. We've a party in a couple of hours. It's not every day that someone is four years old."

"Okay, Melvin. You're so bossy. I always thought Nan was the boss in your relationship."

"Relationship? What's all that about? We're just companions. Isn't that right, Miriam?"

Miriam smiled as she and Amy went to get ready for the party, but as she walked past Melvin she couldn't help herself whispering in his ear.

"If you aren't careful, Melvin, we can always go back to being just companions in separate bedrooms. Is that what you want?"

Up at the shop Edelina was running through a few things with Marco, while Heather had gone to collect the birthday cake from the bakery. They were both excited as having little Rex in their lives was very special to both of them.

"So, Marco, the Dutch lady said she'll come back for the white trousers and pink top this afternoon. I've left them on the table in the workroom. Oh, and there should be a delivery of sandals coming either today or tomorrow. If you want, you can make a display. I've left the price tags on the table, so I think that's everything."

"Miss Edelina, just go and have some fun. I'll be fine. I've been working here for nearly two years now and there's nothing I don't know about running the shop. I love every minute of it. It's my stage! Darling, today I'll give a fabulous performance and take lots of money."

"I know you will. Employing you was the best business decision Heather and I made. The customers love you."

"Yes, and it's the best job I've ever had. To think all those years playing with my sister's Sindy dolls, dressing them up, and now here I am dressing up real ladies up and making them look fabulous. It's every gay man's dream job. Hello, Miss Heather. I was just saying how lucky I am to have this fabulous job."

"Good morning, Marco. I've brought you a couple of pastries from the bakery to keep you going through the day."

"Oh, thanks, but no thanks. I can't be eating pastries. I need to make sure I look my best for next week. You know it's when all the Italians come to Holkamos. I need to find me a rich classy man who'll just want to wine and dine me. Oh, and spend lots of money on me."

"You are funny, Marco. Have a good day. Phone us if there're any problems."

"I'll have a fabulous day. I wonder who'll be first through the door to have a Marco makeover."

Everything was ready for the party. Little Rex was in his new outfit, the food was all prepared, the garden was decorated with bunting and balloons and it looked just like an English village fete. Heather and Edelina were the first to arrive and Rex was so excited.

"Grandma, look. Come and see my presents. Melvin has put balloons in the trees and we have jelly."

Amy and Paul stood at the end of the garden watching Rex with his two grandmothers. It was so lovely to see.

"I'm really happy, Amy. You know that, don't you? It's not just Rex that makes my life perfect. It's you as well. You know, there was a time when I thought I'd lost you, a time when I wasn't the fella for you. That ring was so important to you and you could have chosen Andréas."

"That stupid ring. I should have taken it off the day he told me he loved Katia. There was never a choice. I loved you and love you even more now."

"Oh, talking of Andréas, here they are now. To think I was so jealous of the two of you, but look at us now. We're like one big happy family now we've got to know them. Their children are like cousins to Rex. We're very lucky."

The party got under way and the food was great as Melvin and Miriam had put on a marvellous spread. The children ran around, playing in the garden. This was a perfect summer's day on the island. As it started to get dark, all the lights came on in the garden and everyone relaxed. This was what Volmos was all about, family and friends having fun, eating, drinking and enjoying one another's company.

"Did you ever think we'd be here in this garden watching our children playing, Amy? I do hope they enjoy their childhood as much as we enjoyed ours. We did make the right decision five years ago, didn't we? You don't have any regrets?"

"No regrets, Andréas. Definitely no regrets."

It wasn't just a birthday party for Rex, but also a very special time for everyone. It was late, all the guests had left and Paul was putting Rex to bed. Edelina and Melvin had insisted on clearing everything away.

"Come on, you two. While it's nice and quiet, let's walk off all that food and drink. I want to see the sea."

Heather, Amy and Miriam took the short walk down on to Volmos beach and as they got nearer they saw people getting off the sea taxis coming back from a night in Holkamos town. The boats and yachts anchored out to sea were lit up and it all looked so beautiful and peaceful. They walked down to the water's edge, looking out at the moon shining onto the water.

"Did I make the right decision bringing us back here after all those years? Of course, I did. This is where we have so many happy memories. This beautiful island was a big part of our lives and will be for many years to come."

"Yes, you did, Nan. Mum and I can never thank you enough for bringing us back here. It doesn't really matter whether they're memories or secrets as long as we have each other and we're happy. That's all that really counts, don't you think?"

"Yes, darling, you're right. Perhaps from now on I won't use the word 'secret' any more, just memories."

Chapter 19

Miriam and Melvin enjoyed a quiet few days after Amy, Paul and Rex returned home. The house seemed so still with no little boy running around. They both missed their families once they returned to England, although Melvin's grandchildren were a lot older and seemed to spend the whole holiday on their phones, but it was still lovely to have them stay. Melvin had gone to make a cup of tea. He was gone ages and Miriam was beginning to think he had gone to pick the leaves.

"I thought you'd got lost. I was going to send out a search party."

"No, I just answered the phone. It was Mrs Jackson who called. They are the family who are arriving in the holiday let next week for a month. She called to cancel as they've had a death in the family. She offered to pay, but I told her we'd still be able to let the house out as it's peak season.

"Oh dear, what a shame for them, but to be honest, Melvin, it will be a break for us if it doesn't get let out. Like you said the other week, we're getting a little too old to be turning that house around every few weeks."

"Yes, I know you're right, darling. We do need to give it some serious thought, but not now. I need to drink this tea and then get ready for Edelina and Heather. I'm going to cook pork chops and sauté potatoes."

"Are you sure you don't want me to cook?"

"No, you three women can catch up on all the fashion and jewellery news."

Up at the shop Edelina and Heather were waiting for Marco to arrive as he was covering the shop while they went down to Volmos for dinner. They were both a bit nervous as they wanted to ask him a favour. Edelina was sure he would accept their offer, but would it fit in with his busy social life?

"Good afternoon, Marco. How are you today?"

"Don't ask. I'm not saying a word, but if you really want me to tell you, I will. I've finished with men altogether. They're full of stupid promises. I've washed my hands of them, so don't ask any more."

After another 15 minutes of Marco going on and on about an Italian holidaymaker who had stood him up for a younger model, they managed to calm him down and explain their proposition. He jumped at it, like the cat that got the cream. He was so excited and planning outfits for different times of the day.

There was no such excitement at Carolina's, just doom and gloom. She knew the day would arrive at some point, but it was something she was dreading telling Andréas. He wouldn't be happy, but there was nothing that any of them could do about it.

"Hello, girls. Come through. Miriam's in the garden. Is that champagne I see? Are we celebrating something? You go on out and I'll fetch some glasses."

Once the champagne was poured, Heather explained her exciting news. They had been approached by a chain of fashion shops on all the big Greek islands to supply them with jewellery. They were both so happy. It would mean traveling to the island and back once a month and Marco had agreed to work extra hours in the shop. During the winter months they hoped to be able to build up their stock. Miriam and Melvin were so happy for them both. They had a lovely evening and even Amy joined in on Skype.

Andréas and the rest of the staff knew something was the matter. His uncle, Giorgio, had asked all the staff to stay behind for a little chat after the customers had left. Just like his mother, Andréas knew what was coming as it had been on the cards for a few months.

"Thank you for staying behind. I've something to tell you all, but before I say anything I want you to know that you're all like family to me. Several of you have worked with me for many years and have been so loyal. When other restaurants have offered you jobs, you've stuck by me and I appreciate every one of you. As you're all aware I've not been too well this season and the doctors have told me I need to slow down. At some point I might need a little operation on my heart, so I'm going to Athens for some tests. I'll be away for a few months, but all your jobs are safe. While I'm away, my son, Nico, is coming home to Holkamos to take over the restaurant. I'm sure you'll all give him the help and support that you've given me."

Chapter 20

BUCKINGHAMSHIRE, ENGLAND

"Mum, come quickly. I've got it! We'll open it together. You're on the cover. Hurry up. This is so exciting. Can you really believe we're all in the top celebrity magazine in the country?"

"Okay. Calm down, Cleo. I'm just as excited as you."

Sarah and Cleo sat in the morning room and slowly turned the pages. There on Page 11 was the first photograph with the huge headline.

Lord Ferngate throws a 50th birthday party for his beautiful wife, Lady Sarah Ferngate, at their stunning 60-room home. Everyone from royalty and members of the government were invited to help celebrate the occasion.

As Cleo and Sarah turned the pages they looked at different things. Sarah was so proud of the magnificent hall. Years of hard work had resulted in such a stunning place. On the other hand, Cleo was looking at the clothes, dresses from all the top designers. The magazine had captured the evening so perfectly. After an hour of going over and over the photos, Cleo left to catch the train to London. This was a wonderful opportunity for everyone to see her. She couldn't wait for people to say, "Isn't that the girl in the magazine?" For Sarah, it was a quiet day going over all her charity paperwork and dozens of emails with her secretary, but first of all a walk in the grounds to clear her head.

"Lots to go through today, Tina. What will you choose first? Invitation or the emails?"

"First of all, I think you should see this. It's only just been sent, but I'm a little worried and I don't know why."

It was from one of the big red top papers and wasn't the usual email asking for an opinion or requesting an interview on one of the charities. This seemed urgent as the journalist was most insistent that she spoke to Lady Ferngate today. After a few phone calls, Sarah agreed to see the journalist.

Four hours later Sarah stood at the door watching the so-called journalist drive away. This was the first time in her 50 years that she didn't know what to do. Who could help her? She needed time to think, but more importantly she needed to hide. She had two days before the story would be all over the newspapers and the Internet.

Chapter 21

"Melvin, it's the phone. Stephen wants a word with you. He's on the way. We're really looking forward to you all coming out next month. Here he is, Stephen, Love to everyone. Bye for now."

"Hello, son. Is everything all right? This is a strange time for you to be phoning."

After putting the phone down, Melvin went back to Miriam in the garden and explained that a very old friend of Stephen's needed somewhere to stay for a while. She wasn't in hiding, but needed somewhere very private, away from England, so she was going to stay in the holiday house for a while. Melvin was going to pick her up from Preveza Airport later, but Stephen had asked that they didn't tell anyone she was here.

"This is all very strange, Melvin. Do you know her and why all the secrets?"

"Oh yes, Miriam. I've known her for years. She's lovely. She and Stephen are really good friends, but the thing is you know of her as well. This isn't going to be easy, my darling. We're going to have to be very careful not to let the cat out of the bag. Our guest is none other than Lady Sarah Ferngate."

Over in the harbour, Andréas and his work colleagues all had a night to sleep on the news. Not one of them was happy about it. They had all met or worked with Nico and they all held the same opinion of him. He was spoilt and lazy and had never done a day's work in his life. He had just gone from one Greek island to another partying and enjoying the money that his father sent him every month. However, there was nothing they could do about it. The season still had three months left to go and for Giorgio's sake, they just had to stick it out.

While Melvin went to collect their new guest, Miriam gave the holiday let a good dust and bought some essential groceries. It also gave her time to ponder over the new arrival. Why would someone with such a high profile be hiding down here on Volmos beach? Something was wrong? What was it about Holkamos and secrets?

Heather was busy putting together several collections of the jewellery. She and Edelina were off to Crete, Corfu and Zante in just over a week and so she needed to get on with the task. Edelina was busy unpacking some new stock. It was an exciting time for both of them and their business and they were looking forward to all the island hopping and taking time out for each other. Life was very good. No, their life together was very special.

Melvin stood at the arrivals gate waiting for Sarah to come through customs. He tried to remember the last time he saw her. It was at Pearle's funeral as both she and Lord Ferngate had come. They had both said such lovely things about Pearle. Sarah was such a confident person. Even all those years ago when Stephen brought her to stay, Melvin had always thought they would make a good couple, but Pearle had thought otherwise. She always said that there was only one thing on Sarah's agenda and that was success. Pearle was right. Sarah had turned out to be a very powerful woman. It seemed ages before anyone who resembled her came through the door, it was mostly families and couples, a few Greek businessmen and an elderly scruffy lady. That was it. Perhaps she wasn't coming after all. With that the scruffy woman walked towards him. Oh, what a state she looks now, Melvin thought to himself.

"Hello, Melvin. I can't thank you enough for letting me stay. You're so kind."

"It's so lovely to see you, Lady Ferngate."

"Please, Melvin, call me Sarah."

The journey from Preveza Airport to getting off the ferry was a bit tense, but once on Holkamos Sarah started to relax. Melvin refrained from asking questions and just talked about the island, pointing out various things as he drove along the winding roads. He didn't want to put Sarah in the awkward position of having to talk about her family. As Miriam had said, it was none of their business why she was here. They didn't ask personal details from other paying guests, so they didn't need to know Sarah's. Saying that though, Melvin knew Miriam very well, and he was certain that it wouldn't be long before she found out everything.

"Here we are. You just go through that gate and I'll bring in the luggage. Miriam's waiting for us."

"Hello, you must be Miriam. Thank you so much. I hope you've not gone to too much trouble on my behalf. I'm so grateful for all you've both done."

Miriam could tell that this was a very troubled woman and she wasn't going to bombard Sarah with lots of questions. Well, not yet. She showed her around the little house and suggested that Sarah write a shopping list so that tomorrow they would get everything she needed. After about half an hour, they said their goodbyes and left.

"Melvin, that is a very troubled soul who looks to be at breaking point to me. She seems so fragile. We need to ensure we do everything we can to protect her."

Sarah was not the only new arrival on Holkamos. She may have been frail, nervous and shy, but the other new arrival was completely the opposite – confident, brash and full of their own importance.

"Hi, Andréas. Still only a waiter and still stuck in this

dump of a restaurant? Well, I'm here now and changes are about to happen. I'll be injecting a bit of life into this restaurant. No, I'm going to bring in some fun and excitement to Holkamos. It's goodbye to the old and hello to the new."

"Hello, Nico. Welcome back to Holkamos. We've been waiting for you."

"Waiting for me, yes, but not looking forward to it I bet. Please tell me that's not Angelo? Is he still here after all these years? Well I'm telling you something, you might just about fit into my new project, but its curtains for him."

With that off Nico went to find Giorgio. The staff looked at each other and all had the same opinion. They just had to get through the rest of the summer, earn as much as they could and look for something else for next year.

Chapter 22

The next few days on the island were much the same as usual, although several people knew there were changes on the way. Some were nervous and others very excited. Marco was at the top of that list as he was going to be running Edelina's shop by himself for four days. In his mind, he considered it to be his own shop and by the end of the fourth day women from all over the island would be flocking in to have the famous Marco treatment. Both Heather and Edelina knew they were leaving the shop in good hands or perhaps they should say excitable hands!

"Right then, Marco. Any problems, just phone one of us and if you get tired just close early. Is there anything you'd like to ask?"

"Go, girls! Go and have fun! I'm so jealous you're off to those fabulous islands, full of hot men but then that won't interest you two. Perhaps you could bring me back one though!"

"I thought you were finished with men."

"Oh, that was earlier in the week. I'm over that now. It's time for fun."

The staff at Giorgio's restaurant were anxious. Nothing had changed yet; Nico only popped in to eat and drink. Yes, he certainly liked to drink. The following week he would be taking over as his dad was then going to be flying to Athens to see a heart specialist. No doubt life would be very different then.

Over on Volmos Miriam had only spoken to Sarah twice when she had given her some groceries, but most of the time she could see Sarah reading in the garden. She knew she ought to broach the subject of why Sarah was here. She didn't really want to, but it was only fair because it was all over the British press and probably the Internet too. Miriam gathered up the six newspapers she had bought, and taking a bottle of wine with her, she went to see Sarah.

"Hello, Miriam. Please come in. Judging by what you have there, I presume you know why I'm here."

"No, I don't. It's none of my business and to be honest I bought them because I thought you would want to read them. Knowing what the Press is like, I expect most of it is lies and rubbish. I also brought something enjoyable for you. A nice bottle of red."

"Have you got time to sit and have a glass with me? You and Melvin have been so kind to me, so it's only fair that I explain why you're hiding me here, because that is what it is. I'm in hiding."

They went into the garden and Sarah told Miriam all about her special party, the magazine and then the journalist arriving. That's when she announced the dreadful news. A woman, who had seen the magazine, was very angry. She had been Lord Ferngate's mistress for 15 years and wanted more from him. He paid for her flat and all her living expenses, but once she saw those photos she wanted more. She wanted him permanently instead of the two or three nights a week when he was in London? Why should she not be able to spend Christmases and birthdays with him? Seeing the photos pushed her over the edge. She took photos, receipts and as much evidence as she could find to sell her story to the Press. That's when the journalist told Sarah everything.

"Miriam, I didn't have a clue. Not once throughout my marriage did I ever think there was someone else? I've not seen him. I just needed to get away to think and plan. I know I'm not the guilty party, but that's how I feel. Apart from you, Melvin and Stephen, no one else knows I'm here. I've talked to my two children. They know I'm safe, but don't know where. I need to sort it out without anyone giving me advice."

"Oh dear, poor you. I assure you I won't be giving you any words of wisdom, but all I will say is that I'm here if you need me. We're both here for you. Neither of us are in a position to give advice, but we just want you to enjoy your stay here on the island."

Over the next few hours they chatted about families and the island. In fact, everything apart from Sarah's problem. Her phone was switched off and that's the way she intended it to stay.

"Talking of Stephen, they were good times. We had so many happy times together before I met my husband. We partied hard but saying that we also worked hard."

"How did you meet each other? I would think you both came from two completely different backgrounds. I love Stephen dearly, but I can't imagine him mixing in the circles you did. His background was more working men's clubs, snooker and rugby, whereas I would think yours was finishing school and cocktail parties in the House of Lords."

"You must be joking, Miriam. I was brought up in a little mining town in Derbyshire. We didn't have two pennies to rub together. Well, that's a lie. Both my parents worked hard and we had food, clothes and holidays. They might have only been to Skegness, but we were very happy. I was contented and happy until I went on a school trip and everything changed. I was on a mission and no one was going to stop me. I succeeded but look at me now. I'm almost back to stage one, no home, no confidence, and this time round I haven't even got youth on my side. I'm fifty and homeless."

"I know I said I'm in no position to give advice, but I do know we've drunk too much wine! You're not too old at all. You're a very clever woman who's done nothing wrong apart from love your family and a husband who's cheated on you. There'll be a light at the end of the tunnel, you mark my words. With that, I think it's time I went home. Just promise me one thing. If you need anything or someone to chat to, just knock on the door."

"Thank you, Miriam. I'm so grateful. I just don't want to become a burden."

Chapter 23

Back from their island hopping, both Heather and Edelina were busy with the orders for the new shops. They were happy because the shop owners who had bought the jewellery were so excited about next year's items that they wanted to go all out with a big launch in May. This would give Heather all winter to prepare for it. While they were away, Marco had sold a lot of stock and was over the moon with his new window display.

"Oh, Marco, I think we need to leave the window for you to do. That looks fabulous. I never would have thought to put those items together like that. They look so good."

"Edelina, I was thinking. Seeing as though most of the holiday makers come to the island for two weeks, we should change the window weekly, to attract more interest. Perhaps one week have more clothes, and the next week more accessories. What do you think?"

"I think I should leave it to you."

Down at the harbour the staff in the restaurant were dreading the day. Giorgio had gone to Athens to see his doctors and Nico was now in charge. He had called a meeting of all the waiters and kitchen staff and showed them his plans for the restaurant, glossy photographs and menus.

"In a nutshell, I'm bringing Mikonos to Holkamos. No more of this boring, quiet life. I'm going to go for the hip youngsters. This is going to be a fun place with a new look, new menus, new everything."

The staff knew exactly what he meant. They were on the way out. Andréas was angry. This had been a successful family business for many generations. It didn't need any changes. Visitors come back year after year, it made money and everyone was happy. Angelo had walked away as this new concept wasn't for him. He had worked for Giorgio for 30 years, even before Nico was born, and had been so grateful to the family for taking him in when he arrived from Athens as a young man. They had taught him everything and treated him as one of their family. He didn't know what he was going to do now. Holkamos was his life and more importantly the little room above the restaurant had been his home for all those years. He didn't just need to find a job, he also needed to find a home. The staff kept telling him that Giorgio wouldn't allow him to be treated badly, but he knew that blood was a lot thicker than water and in Giorgio's view, Nico could do no wrong. The future was looking very bleak.

Stephen had phoned to see how Sarah had settled in. He had spotted a journalist outside his house, looking to see whether she was staying with him. Melvin reassured him that Sarah was just another holiday maker on the island, as she hadn't left the house during the week, perhaps they should try and encourage her to walk down to the beach. Miriam suggested she should invite her round for a meal and also invite Heather and Edelina. It would be a start.

After the meeting Andréas made an excuse to go out. He needed to go back up to Creakos to tell his mother the news and he also hoped it would calm him down. He was worried that Carolina would be upset as it was the restaurant where her father had been for all those years as well as her beloved grandfather. However, her reaction wasn't one which Andréas was expecting. Carolina just laughed and laughed.

"Oh dear, Andréas. What a fool he is. One modern restaurant on Holkamos isn't going to turn the island into another Mykonos. The visitors who come here come because they love the old Greece with its peace and quiet. They don't want a party island. I suggest you just keep quiet and watch Nico fall flat on his face. Everyone's been telling my brother for years that his son's a lazy sponger. What more can we do? He thinks the sun shines out of him. You mark my words. When the season starts again next year, Nico'll be long gone."

Andréas could see his mother's point and that made him feel better. He just hoped that he could reassure Angelo and all the other staff that they had to stick together to see this through.

Sarah had accepted Miriam's invitation for dinner. Heather and Edelina were unable to come because of their jewellery orders, but suggested that Marco went. He loved going to chat to Miriam. He was always the life and soul of any party and if the situation was explained to him he would not say a word.

As Miriam and Melvin prepared things in the kitchen, Marco and Sarah chatted in the garden. There was no fear that Marco would ask any awkward questions as the talk was all about him, the excitement of the shop and how he was more like a manager than a shop assistant and had lots of responsibilities. Sitting out in the shade, they enjoyed their food and Sarah seemed very relaxed. Marco had no idea who she was. He believed her to be just another holiday maker staying on Volmos.

"So, Marco, have you lived here on Holkamos all your life?"

"No, I moved here a few years ago, but I call it home. You see, my so-called family don't approve of me. When I was young they could tell me what to do, but as I got older and realised I was gay that's when the trouble started. I wouldn't play football and cricket and that disappointed my mother and father. They hated the way I dressed and acted and as for my friends, they didn't approve of them either, so when I was old enough I came here. I've done lots of jobs and people accept me for who I am. I don't have to live my life in secret. My family know where I am, but sadly I'm not welcome back on their little island so I've made my home here."

"And we always say that this island is a far better place for having you here, don't we, Melvin? It's never boring and dull when Marco's around. Would anyone like another drink?"

"Not for me, thank you, Miriam. I'm going to catch the last boat back into town. Thank you for a lovely evening, it was so nice to meet you, Sarah. You must come up to the shop while you're here and I'll give you the famous Marco makeover."

"I'll see you out, Marco, and then I'm going to tidy up in the kitchen. You two ladies can sit and chat. I'll leave you with this bottle of red. Enjoy."

"You have such a perfect life, Miriam. It's so simple, no complications and in such a beautiful place, not that I've seen much of it yet. My life could have been simple, but I made it complicated. You see, I was greedy. I wouldn't settle for anything but the best and for the last thirty years I've not stopped. Even when I got what I wanted, I then had to work even harder juggling everything and this last week I've realised how stupid I've been. Don't get me wrong. I love my husband and children, but did I really love the life we had? I thought so, but somehow I think it was all a waste of time and energy."

"No, you can't say that, Sarah. Look at what you've achieved with all your charity work, not to mention how respected you are by so many people. You must be so proud of yourself."

"Miriam, anyone who marries a Lord could have achieved that. Just because I had a title people would suck up to me. No, the only thing I'm proud of is that my two children haven't been spoilt. Yes, they've had an expensive education, but they're honest, hardworking and appreciate everything they have. That's my only real achievement, but I suppose I did fulfil my silly dream. A dream that should never have come true."

"But if you fulfilled your dream, that must be good."

"Yes, that's what I used to think, but mine was a stupid dream. It all started on a school trip. The night before the outing, my mum, dad, sister and I went to my cousin's new Wimpey home. She had just got married and they had only moved in a few weeks previously. Coming away from there I was so jealous of her. That's what I wanted, a husband and a two-up, two-down. It's strange to think that I ended up with sixty rooms. Anyway, the next day the school trip was to Chatsworth House. On the coach I was telling my friend all about the little house and I joked about having three children and a loving husband and going to Skegness every year for our holidays. That little mining town was going to be my life until I died, but then we drove through the huge gates to that magnificent house at Chatsworth. But it wasn't until this little old lady gave us a tour round, that my dream began. She explained that it wasn't just a museum house, a family actually lived there. I couldn't believe it and that was my mission. I wanted a house like that, I wanted to be the Lady of the Manor and no one or nothing was going to stop me."

"Yes, and you achieved it, Sarah. Your dream came true. You should be proud of yourself and if it wasn't for what's happened with your husband, you would still be proud."

"Miriam, I'm beginning to think that my husband's done me a favour. During the time I've been here, I've realised many things. I probably would have wanted more than that little Wimpey house and I expect I would have left that little town. Did that dream fulfil me? I don't think so. Large and great isn't always the best. No, Miriam it's time to rethink things. It's time to perhaps have another dream, a simpler one. Could I ask you something? Would you show me around the island? All this business of me hiding is ridiculous. I'm a fifty-year-old woman whose husband has cheated on her. Who wants to know what I'm doing? It's time to move on and what better way than having a holiday in the sunshine?

Chapter 24

Carolina didn't know what to do. Yes, she knew that Nico's wild ideas would fail with many people being unhappy, but she couldn't contact Giorgio as with all his health issues it would just be another worry. In his eyes, his son was always right but there must be something she could do. Nico wouldn't listen to her, but on the other hand he needed her as a friend and not an enemy.

Down on Volmos, Miriam had explained everything to Melvin and had made arrangements with Sarah to show her around the town and harbour. She was somewhat worried about Sarah being recognised and how she would cope with that, but like Melvin had said, "If it happens, it happens and perhaps it would be good to get it out of the way." Miriam had arranged to meet Sarah at ten-thirty and they planned to walk up to the castle and back down the hill to the harbour for lunch and then catch the sea taxi back during the late afternoon. Melvin was going to spend the day pottering about in the garden or as Miriam called it 'chatting to his cosmos friends'.

Andréas arrived at the restaurant and as usual there was no sign of Nico, so he unlocked everything and began to set things up for the day's business. Next to arrive was Angelo. Andréas knew he would have to reassure him that everything would be alright in the long run and they would just have to go with any changes. There was no way that Giorgio would have him evicted from the accommodation.

"Come on, Angelo. The sun's out and the holiday makers are happy. The last thing they need to see is miserable faces. Let's put some music on and get the show on the road."

Andréas knew that everything was down to him. He needed to hold everything together, not just on behalf of the staff, but also for the family name. This restaurant was his past; a very important part of Holkamos and he was going to ensure that one way or another it would be the future.

Once Miriam had met Sarah at the holiday let, they walked down the lane until they arrived at Volmos beach. It was still early, and people were getting their sunbeds. Miriam suggested they should walk instead of taking the sea taxi. On the way up to the castle, they stopped several times to look back at the view and take it all in.

"It's Paradise, Miriam, that's what it is! I know hundreds of years ago there wouldn't have been sunbeds and things, but if you removed them, to me it just looks like time has stood still and nothing's changed. Oh, I'm so grateful to Stephen for suggesting that I come here."

"You just wait until we reach the top. You can look out over the whole town. It's such an amazing view and one I never get tired of. Do you know what? Every day I count my blessings. My life could easily have taken a very different path, but I'm so happy it didn't. I believe everything happens for a reason. Now come on, we're nearly at the top and I'm getting too sentimental."

They finally arrived at the top and headed towards the castle gates. Just like all the visitors, they sat on the little wall looking down into the harbour. Miriam could tell by the look on Sarah's face that she was overwhelmed with the view. She did not have to say a word. After a 15-minute silence, Sarah eventually spoke.

"It looks to me as though the harbour curves are a

pair of arms opening out, calling you in for a hug. Isn't it so welcoming! Oh yes, Miriam. I can see why you love it so much. This is Greece at its very best."

Before they started to walk down the hill and call in on Heather and Edelina, they stopped off at one of the little restaurants for coffee and sat looking down towards the town. Sarah got out her phone and took some photos and after checking which were the best ones, she looked at Miriam.

"I think it's time to let my children know I'm safe and tell them where I am. Well, I might just forget to say which island I'm on, but at least they'll know where in the world I am."

"Why don't I take a photo of you, so that they can see you really are alright?"

"That's kind of you, but I don't think I'm quite ready for that yet. Perhaps another time."

With coffee over, they had a quick chat and introduction with Heather and Edelina. Thankfully Marco wasn't there or they would have been there for hours, with him giving Sarah the Marco makeover. They took a look at Heather's new jewellery designs, and then strolled down past all the little shops, restaurants and the bakery and finally arrived at the harbour. By this time it wasn't too busy as most people were on the beaches enjoying the beautiful weather. Sarah had received two texts back from her children, but she didn't reply. They knew she was safe and well and that's all that mattered.

Over the next couple of hours they walked along the water's edge and up and down the little side streets. Sarah was really interested in the history of Holkamos and Miriam was eager to tell her all about it to take her mind away from everything she had left behind in England. They talked about the small church on the island and Miriam also mentioned the church down on Volmos beach as someone tapped her on the shoulder.

It was Carolina. After introductions and general chitchat, Miriam suggested that Carolina should join them for a late lunch, which was perfect as she wanted to tell her about Nico's arrival and his plans for the restaurant.

"Well, what a perfect opportunity for us to go and see what's happening, Carolina. You never know we might be drinking cocktails instead of our normal carafe of red wine."

Andréas greeted them and showed them to a table. There was still no sign of Nico and everything was just the same as usual. Andréas explained that one of the chefs had seen Nico go off with a female holidaymaker the previous night, and they had all come to the conclusion that he was still with her. Carolina was a lot like Miriam and wanted to know what had brought Sarah to the island and why she was by herself. Miriam was poised to jump in and rescue the situation, but there was no need. Sarah explained that she and her husband had split up and she was having a few weeks away to consider her options. Her children were now adults and they didn't need her, so it was now time to make a new start for herself. It was all very convincing and to be honest it was the truth. Perhaps not the whole truth, but none of it was a lie.

Over the next hour or so they talked about their families, children and life on the island. Carolina was pleased to have bumped into them as she wanted to see the atmosphere in the restaurant. Just like Andréas she was very worried about Angelo. He was more like family to her than many of her real family, and she was surprised how chirpy he was as he chatted to them, welcomed Sarah to the island and really fussed over them. They enjoyed a lovely lunch together and Sarah insisted on paying the bill. As she was doing so, Miriam went to the toilet and Carolina sat looking out to sea. She noticed Nico walking towards the restaurant and thought to herself: the only way to win this is to let him think we're on his side.

"Hello, Aunt Carolina. How are you? It's so very nice to see you. Have you got time for a chat? I've got so much to tell you."

"No, I'm sorry, Nico, but I'm out with two friends. We've just had a lovely lunch here, but we need to get going. By the way, welcome back to Holkamos. It's so good to see you here on the island. Andréas has told us all about your exciting new plans and it's good that the lady or girl that I saw you with last night seemed so willing to help you. I expect you've had a busy morning. Oh, its four-thirty already. I mean, busy day working on all the plans together. Here are my friends. No doubt, I'll catch up with you again soon."

Nico wasn't able to get a word in edgeways. "That's one up to me," Carolina said to herself. She may have come out on top with that one, but sadly she knew that was just the first of many conversations she needed to win. As they said goodbye, Miriam and Sarah headed for the sea taxi. What a lovely day they'd had, and now Sarah had got her bearings there would be no stopping her exploring by herself. Back on Volmos they strolled back to the house. Sarah declined Miriam's offer of dinner with her and Melvin, saying that she was tired and wanted to write some emails. She thanked her for a lovely day and said that it would be lovely to do it again some time.

"Just one thing, Miriam. I was wondering how long I could rent the house from you, as I'm beginning to think I might be here for quite a while."

"I'm not sure without looking in the diary, but I know it will be alright for at least eight weeks. Stephen and his family are coming over and they usually stay there, but that's not a problem as they can stay with us. I'll let you know the situation after that. Thank you for today. I've really enjoyed showing you around parts of this lovely island. I hope I've helped to take your mind off things, but if you need anything or just fancy a chat, you know where I am."

Chapter 25

Over the next few days Sarah went out and about by herself with any thought of being recognised far from her mind. She was enjoying having a little break in the sunshine, but most of all she was loving her own company. This was so new to her as all her life she had been part of a team. When she was young it had been her family, then her working life and married life. All this was strange to her. It was new, and as much as she loved her children, she was really enjoying her own company. She knew it would all have to come to an end sometime, but now she was making the most of it.

Sarah wasn't the only one enjoying her holiday. From what Andréas and the staff could see, all Nico was doing was having a good time and he was never in the restaurant. The staff were all thankful for this, life was ticking along quite happily, although Carolina continued to warn Andréas. Nico might be out and about having fun, but it wouldn't last forever.

Miriam and Melvin enjoyed having Sarah living next door to them as she was quiet and fended for herself. Consulting the diary, they confirmed that there was just two weeks in September where they needed the holiday let, but after that Sarah could rent it for as long as she wanted.

"Miriam, I've got your note with the dates on. Thank you so much. I'm so pleased. I'll move out for those two weeks, no problem. You have both been so kind to me, I can't thank you enough. One other thing, would it be alright if my daughter came to stay for a week? I've told her where I am and she's worried about me."

"Of course. That's not a problem, Sarah. You can invite whoever you like. It's your house to do whatever you want with. Anyway, what have you been up to lately, anything nice? Have you been to the beach?"

Sarah told Miriam about the time she spent over the last few days and that she had taken her advice and caught the water taxi from Volmos to Holkamos town at night.

"Oh, you were so right, Miriam. It's magical. As the sea taxi pulls away from the castle, there in front of you is the town all lit up with the lights flickering in the water. It's very special, but I'm trying to walk as much as possible as I can feel the weight going on. I've been back to that same restaurant every day and even twice in one day."

"Oh, good. Andréas is a lovely boy. I hope he looked after you."

"Yes, he was there, but one of the other waiters always made sure I was alright. Angelo, was so helpful, giving me snippets of information about the island and places to see. He also made sure I had a table with a great view, so yes, I felt very comfortable there. Today I thought I'd walk up to your daughter's shop and treat myself to some new clothes. I'm sure I'll get the Marco makeover! Thanks again, Miriam. Have a lovely day."

"Hello, Sarah. I've been expecting you. I knew you'd come up and since we had dinner at Miriam's and Melvin's I've been putting together a collection of clothes I thought you may like. Come in and have a look. I've started with the basic white and added pieces with colour for day and night. Pinks, yellows and gorgeous lime greens."

For the next two hours Marco had Sarah trying on the whole collection and to her surprise she loved it. He really had given a lot of thought to it, creating a casual, fresh new look which was completely different to anything she had ever worn before. Apart from a few things which she thought were perhaps too young for her, Sarah decided to buy everything. Seven hundred euros worth, to be precise. On their return from Preveza, Edelina and Heather would be so pleased. Marco had said that he would arrange for Edelina to drop the clothes down to her on Volmos so she wouldn't have to carry them around all day.

"Wait until my daughter sees all of this. She'll want to know what's come over me. We're going to have such fun. Oh, I didn't tell you. She's coming to stay with me for a week. You must meet her. She'll love you. Perhaps you can take her out and show her where all the young people meet up."

"That would be lovely, but here on the island all ages mix and enjoy things together. I'm afraid it's not Mykonos. Well, not yet. There are rumours we're going to have a hip new bar, but things take a long time to change."

Sarah said her goodbyes and thanked Marco for all his hard work in putting everything together. She couldn't wait to wear her new clothes. Marco loved his job and making people happy. He knew it was more than just the clothes. It was about feeling appreciated, something he hadn't encountered as a child.

Slowly strolling down to harbour. Sarah was beginning to feel as if though she belonged there rather than just being a holidaymaker. Trying on all her new clothes had given her an appetite and she was hungry, so she headed down to the little restaurant and sat at her favourite table. She sensed there was a different atmosphere, although everything seemed to be the same as usual apart from a scruffy young chap with a tape measure. Angelo didn't seem to be at all happy and didn't speak to Sarah. However, Sarah was pleased to be in such a special place, looking out to sea. As she did so, a text from Cleo, her daughter, came through with her arrival times. Sarah wondered how she would feel about coming. Would she forgive her father? Was he sorry, saying "Let's turn the clock back to before the party?" No, this wasn't the case. He wasn't sorry at all. He had sent two emails apologising for humiliating her, but not about cheating on her. Sarah knew there was no going back to being a happy family. This was a fresh start and so far she was enjoying the peace and quiet of her freedom on this beautiful island.

Instead of catching the boat back to Holkamos after her wine and Greek salad, Sarah decided to walk the long way back on the top road. She had only ever been this way by car but as it was quite high up, she wanted to see the stunning view. She paid her bill and Andréas apologised for any interruptions.

"Miss Sarah, Miss Sarah. Excuse me."

She turned round and saw Angelo rushing towards her."

"What is it, Angelo? Have I forgotten something?"

"No, Miss Sarah. I wanted to say sorry for being rude today and not making you feel welcome. I'm really sorry. It was so wrong of me."

"Oh, don't be silly. You weren't rude, just not quite yourself. It's nothing to apologise for. I've had yet another lovely meal. Thank you, I really have."

With that they both smiled and went their separate ways. The walk back was a lot longer and more difficult than she had anticipated. At the very top there was a seat looking out over the town with a wonderful view above the trees. It was well worth the journey. The breathtaking view made both Holkamos and Volmos look so large. Sarah turned to walk towards Volmos and saw Carolina coming down the other road. They had a brief chat about how Sarah was enjoying her stay and Cleo's holiday. Sarah mentioned her lunch, she had seen Andréas and what a lovely restaurant it was.

"Yes, but sadly if my nephew has his way, it will soon be a modern bar and that's not really what we want here in Holkamos."

"Oh, that explains why someone was measuring up."

"Oh dear, it's started then. Perhaps it's time for me to pay a visit. I do need to call in and collect the week's paperwork and takings as I'm sorting it all out while my brother's in hospital. He trusts his son to run the restaurant, but he doesn't have a lot of faith in Nico paying wages and suppliers. You must come up and visit us in Creakos. Bring your daughter too. I'll arrange something with Melvin and Miriam. Bye for now."

Sarah really did feel as though she belonged here as people were so friendly. I'm beginning to think that my husband has done me a favour, she thought to herself. If he hadn't cheated on me, I'd never have come to this island. Rather than being the loser in the situation, Sarah was definitely the winner.

When Heather and Edelina returned from Preveza, Marco was giddy with excitement. He had had his best day's takings as apart from Sarah's purchases, he had also sold shoes, bags and lots of jewellery. He was pleased with himself and also delighted for the shop. Edelina couldn't thank him enough and decided to give him ten percent of everything he had sold. Marco was over the moon. It meant he could buy a new outfit to go out in when flirting with all the hunky Italian holiday makers.

That evening Carolina could not believe her eyes. None of the restaurant paperwork made any sense as it was so muddled up. She didn't know where to start. Customer receipts and bills were mixed in with supplier's invoices which needed to be paid and there were also receipts from other businesses for food, clothes and even cigarettes. Carolina needed a plan; this was going to take ages to sort out. So she cleared the kitchen table and put everything in date order, and then arranged each day's paperwork into customer bills and supplier bills. Five hours later she had a very long statement of incomings and outgoings, but she couldn't get her head around it. Had she made a mistake? She didn't want to worry her brother with it, but this was the height of the summer season and more money was going out than coming in. What had she done wrong, but more importantly how could she put it right? By now it was getting late. She would sleep on it as Andréas had enough on his mind and she didn't want to worry him.

Chapter 26

Sarah was up early. She was excited but a little nervous as Cleo was arriving. Although she couldn't wait to see her daughter, she didn't want to answer questions about her marriage. As far as she was concerned, it was over. He had made his choice and she wasn't part of it. Sarah was ready to create a new life for herself although what exactly that entailed, she was yet to discover. Melvin was taking her to Preveza to meet Cleo which was so kind of him. Both he and Miriam were becoming such good friends. They lived such a relaxed and simple life, no trying to keep up with the Joneses type of thing with them. There was no competitiveness, with who's got what and how to climb the social ladder. Sarah contemplated all those wasted years of aiming to be something or somebody, but enough of that, back to today!

Carolina also had things on her mind. Even though she was collecting the paperwork for the restaurant every day, she still couldn't understand any of it. Heather had agreed to look over it all as she carried out bookkeeping for a living. Carolina hoped things would sort themselves out as she didn't want to burden her brother with it. He was still in Athens preparing for a major heart operation. Nico, his son, seemed to be unconcerned about his father's health, as from what she could gather from Andréas, the only thing on Nico's mind was entertaining single female holiday makers. The staff realised he wasn't pulling his weight, but at least he was out of their way.

"Oh, thank you so much, Melvin. I really don't know

what I would have done without you and Miriam. I have Stephen to thank for all this. He's been such a good friend to me over the years. I know we grew apart as he couldn't be doing with all social scene I was involved with, but I still think that apart from having my children, the time Stephen and I worked together was one of the happiest times of my life. We had such fun. We'd be out partying and go straight to work without going home first. They were good times."

"Yes, he's a good lad. I'm very proud of him and his family. There was a time after Pearle died and Miriam moved in, when he could have been very critical but he wasn't. He just wanted me to be happy, that's all."

"I know what you mean. I can still remember the conversation I had with him two hours before I got married. There was I, off to marry a Lord in Saint Paul's Cathedral and he said, "You know you don't have to go through with this. You can walk away." He knew my dream, the dream that had been with me for so many years, the dream he knew was wrong. Perhaps I should have listened to him. God, could you imagine the scandal. Lord Ferngate stood up at the aisle by a waitress."

"Yes, Sarah, but you wouldn't have had your two children. Also think of all the hard work and money which has been raised for your charities. No, you've just come to a crossroad in your life. It's no good looking back, as it's history now. It can't be changed. It's time for the next dream."

"Oh, Melvin. That's such a lovely way of putting it. I think I'll just have to stay on Holkamos until I've had that dream."

Carolina had spent an hour with Heather going through the paperwork for the restaurant. Money in, money out, daily takings – they had gone through everything.

"Well, Carolina, I think you've done a perfect job

with the bookkeeping. You know as well as I do that Nico has been spending the restaurant's money."

Edelina had just told Marco her news and yet again he was giddy with excitement to think that she trusted his opinion on buying for the shop. Thank goodness she had given him plenty of time to research everything.

"Edelina, please repeat what you've just said. I really can't believe it." I really can't believe what you've just said."

"Marco, I'd like you to come to Athens with me in three months' time as we'll be buying next year's summer collections for the shop."

This is the happiest day of my life, he thought to himself. He also realised how important this would be, as there would be a budget and clothes that would sell in big cities wouldn't be appropriate for Holkamos. He needed to put a lot of thought into this, but to think that after all those years of getting his sister to buy outfits he liked for her Sindy dolls, he was now going to be deciding what the ladies on Holkamos will be wearing the following year.

"Here we are, ladies. Welcome to Volmos, Cleo. I hope you have a lovely holiday. Miriam and I are only next door, so just pop in if you need anything."

"Thank you, Melvin. You've done enough for me already. I'm sure we'll manage fine, won't we, Cleo."

"Oh, yes, and thank you for collecting me from the airport. That was very kind of you."

A quick shower for Cleo and as it was getting late, it was off out for some dinner. Sarah was excited for her to see Holkamos from the water taxi at night as it was so beautiful. She was also so pleased that there had been no mention of future plans or even divorce in their conversations. To be honest, the only thing Cleo could talk about was Sarah's new wardrobe of clothes. She loved all of them and couldn't believe how she had ever been persuaded to buy them. She couldn't wait to go and visit the shop, but that would have to wait. Sarah just wanted to reassure her daughter that she was fine, she wasn't unhappy and that actually she was enjoying her new-found freedom.

Miriam was asking Melvin all about Cleo and if Sarah had talked much in the car on the way to the airport. He had come to the conclusion that while the island might be perfect for Sarah, he thought Holkamos would be rather boring for Cleo as she seemed to be the type of girl who liked to have a fun time.

"No, Miriam. I don't think that young lady will be here for very long."

Holkamos was busy, it was the height of the summer season and the restaurants were buzzing with a vibrant atmosphere in the harbour. As the taxi headed into the harbour, Cleo was impressed. She could understand why her mother had fallen in love with the island although she wasn't expecting her to be quite so happy. Her life had just fallen apart and it was just as if she had moved on and putting it bluntly, said goodbye to all those years. However, she wasn't here to tell her mother to come home and try and sort out the problems with her father. She was here to make sure her mum was safe and well and coping with life. It was clear that she was.

"So, what do you want to do? Did you want to go for a little look around or shall we just go for dinner. You choose, it's your holiday."

Cleo chose to walk along the sea wall. They saw a woman selling honey, a man selling corn on the cob and someone painting pictures onto glass. As Cleo turned round, she noticed someone winking at her. He was confident, in his mid-thirties. That was nice, she thought to herself. A few more like that and I'll be having a lovely holiday here.

There was only one restaurant where Sarah wanted to go. The food was good, the service lovely, but not only that they were guaranteed a lovely view of everyone passing by. Andréas was on good form and as they waited for a table to be re-laid, Sarah introduced Cleo to Angelo, Andréas and the other staff. She explained to Cleo that this was her favourite place to eat and how all the staff looked after her. Cleo was beginning to realise that her mother really was starting to make a new life for herself, but was it all happening too quickly?

"Was everything alright? Can I get you another drink?"

"Oh yes, the meal was gorgeous as always, Angelo. Would you like another drink, darling? Some more wine or a coffee?"

"Yes, that would be nice. Could I have a gin and tonic please?"

"And I'll have another glass of red, thank you, Angelo."

"I think he fancies you, Mum. The way he looked at you was different to the way he looked at me."

"Oh, don't be silly, darling. He just knows me better as I eat here most days. All the staff are friendly to me."

"Well, I'm telling you he's got his eye on you. Just be careful. The last thing you need is a relationship."

"Oh, that's what you think. I don't want to argue about this, but all I will say is have you said that to your father?"

Cleo was just about to reply when someone walked up to the table.

"Well, hello again and welcome to my restaurant. I hope you've been well looked after and the food was to your taste."

"I'm sorry, but I don't think we've met. Should I remember you?"

"Sorry, it was meant for the young lady. We smiled at each other earlier in the evening and as I walked away she gave me a look to say she liked what she saw."

Cleo was loving the attention and yes, she did like what she saw, although Sarah definitely didn't. This must be the so-called Nico who'd come back to the island. Angelo returned with the drinks.

"Angelo, get me a whisky and soda. I'm joining these two young ladies for a drink and please take their drinks off the bill. They're on me."

Sarah could see from Angelo's face that he was so embarrassed. Cleo was relishing the attention. This needed to stop before it got out of hand.

"Oh, excuse me. I'm a little confused. Do you work here and is it commonplace for a complete stranger to just sit down with people having a meal?"

"Mum, we've finished eating and this gentleman owns the restaurant, so I think he's entitled to sit where he likes in his restaurant."

"Oh, darling, sorry. I must have had too much to drink because I thought the owner of this restaurant was seriously ill in hospital and the lovely staff here were working so hard to keep the business going while he's not here. Perhaps we won't have these drinks after all. If you would be so kind, do you think we could get up from this table. Fetch me the bill, and by the way could you make sure these drinks are added to it. Thank you."

Cleo was so embarrassed and Nico didn't know what to say. The only one smiling was Andréas who had overheard the whole conversation. Sarah settled the bill and said goodnight to all the staff. Strangely enough, Nico wasn't around anymore and the incident wasn't mentioned at all on the way back to Volmos. Cleo knew better than to answer her mother back where boys, or in this case, men were concerned, because over the years she had been proved right on more than one occasion.

Later that night back up in Creakos, Andréas told the story to his mother and Katia. They all had a good laugh about it, but as far as the problem with the bookkeeping was concerned, tonight wasn't the right time to worry Andréas with it.

"She's a nice lady, Mum, but I think the daughter's a bit of a handful. She brings a smile to Angelo's face, a smile I've not seen for a long time. I think he quite fancies her."

Chapter 27

Over the next few days Cleo and Sarah spent their days on Volmos beach and the garden in the evenings, enjoying the beautiful weather and relaxing. Sarah really enjoyed cooking with Cleo and together they created some lovely meals to eat outside, which was something that didn't happen a lot in England as their lives were far too busy. Helen, their housekeeper, did most of the meals.

"Mum, can I say something? You're so different now. I've never seen you like this in my whole life. It's not just the casual clothes. I'm not saying it's a bad thing. I love the new you because the more time we spend together, the more I feel happy for you. Throughout my life you've been balancing everything around, from us kids to the staff, charity work to Dad's business interests and all those important dinner parties. I'd just like to say I'm so happy for you. I really am."

"Thank you, darling. I really do feel different, but it was just a natural thing. When I arrived here, I had nothing to plan or worry about, which was a great feeling. I don't know how long it will last, but at the moment I'm enjoying my freedom. It reminds me of when I first left home and moved away. Life was new and exciting. This is just the same. What have I got to look forward to?"

"Where does Dad fit into all of this, or doesn't he?"

"To be honest, the moment I stepped onto that plane to come here, I mentally said goodbye to your father. Perhaps if he had only had a one-night stand or a brief affair, things might have turned out differently, but he's had a mistress for years, so I know there's no future for us anymore."

"I do understand, Mum and I won't mention it again. Tell me about when you first left home. You've never talked about life before Dad and us children. What did you get up to and do with your life then?"

"It was so many years ago that I don't think I can remember too much. After leaving school I went to work in the local Co-op, but I didn't expect that to be forever. I used to chat to the older ladies who worked there about leaving the town and making something of myself. A few of them thought I was mad and thought I considered myself to be better than the rest of them. However, there was woman – I can't remember her name, but I can see her face as clearly as if it were yesterday as every few weeks she came in with a bruise or two. She always said she had walked into a door or tripped on the stairs but we all knew differently. Her husband thought too much of himself and had given her a slap. I felt so sorry for her. You see, in those days nothing really was done about it. You just put up with things like that. It was so sad."

"Is that why you became involved with charities for battered wives and hostels for women?"

"Yes, I think it was. We all have a duty to help those who aren't as fortunate as we are. It wasn't until I left that shop and started working in hotels that I began to have fun and grow up. To be honest, I was living and socialising with fabulous people from all walks of life. We didn't have much money and we worked unsociable hours, but we knew how to have a good time. You'd find it so boring, Cleo, but life before the Internet and mobile phones was far simpler. You made your own fun. I think I always tried to help the underdog. I like things to be fair and honest, but we did play hard and have a lot of fun. A lot of my happier times before you two children came along was spent with Brian."

"Was he an old boyfriend?"

"God, no, darling. Brian was gay. In those days there

was far more hostility shown to gay people, although the hotel industry was a lot more tolerant than other places of employment. Brian and I moved to London. We thought we were so special and we embraced everything the big city had to offer but it was back in the Midlands where we became good friends as a result of one stupid incident. Strangely, it all started because I was trying to help a girl I'd known from school. Her name was Jane and she was a year younger than me. She worked at the hotel too and one morning while I was working a breakfast shift she came into work crying. She had been to a late night drinking club with hotel staff the night before and ended up going back to staff accommodation with a chef who lived in. She left in the early hours of the morning, but as she was walking away from the staff block, she noticed the night manager doing his security checks. So that he wouldn't see her, Jane hid in the chef's changing room. On the wall was a chart with the names of all the chefs and kitchen porters along the top. Down one side was a list of all the girls they'd had sex with together with marks out of ten. I could see why she was so upset and I promised her that I would sort it out before her name appeared on that list. I would add, darling, that my name was never on the list. Oh no, I was on a mission to succeed in life and sleeping with a chef or kitchen porter was not part of my plan.

"Well, I needed to see the chart but how could I get into the changing room without them noticing me? I thought of an obvious way. Each morning at half past ten the head chef had a briefing with his staff, so that's when I did it. My name was on the list but without the reference to anyone sleeping with me. On the bottom of the list was Brian's name with lots of horrible comments. I told him about this and that's when we came up with a scheme to get revenge for all those poor girls. We waited until the next catering meeting which all the waiting and kitchen staff attended. The head chef gave his talk followed by the restaurant manager, and then there was a question and answer session which Brian, being the assistant restaurant manager was in charge of. He told all the heads of departments that they could leave and he would go through everything. He then handed over to me and I explained that I had the results of a little project I had been conducting over the previous six months. The waiting staff were in on this with me, but the chefs looked at me blankly. In top place for the biggest willy was Clive, followed by so and so... This went on until I announced the smallest. And now for performance with marks out of ten. With this, they all got up and walked out. It was weeks before everything returned to normal, but we did laugh about it for a long time. That's when Brian earned the respect of the entire kitchen staff. Gay or not, he wasn't going to allow anyone to demean him."

"But, Mum, how did you end up working and living in London?"

"Oh, that was all down to Brian. He got a promotion with the hotel company and I went with him. That was the beginning of lots of funny stories and also when I first met Stephen, but I'll save that for another time. I think I might have an early night now. How about you?"

"No, I'm not tired. What time's the last water taxi back from Holkamos, Mum? As it's only quite early, I think I might go and have a walk around. You don't mind, do you?"

"Not at all, darling, but make sure that when you get off the sea taxi you ask them what time they finish for the night. You won't want to be walking that big hill."

By the time Cleo had got ready and arrived in the harbour it was half past ten and the place was buzzing with families. As she walked past the restaurants, the aroma of cooking was so enticing, but she wasn't hungry and thought it would be nice to sit and watch everyone walking along the sea front from the little restaurant her mother liked. Andréas recognised her and found her a table in the corner from where she could enjoy the view. Cleo ordered a gin and tonic and just like her mother, she was beginning to fall in love with the island.

Carolina had decided to confront Nico about his spending. For a start there wasn't enough money to pay the staff and suppliers and she didn't have access to draw money from her brother's bank account. She could only pay money in. She would wait until it was nearly time for the restaurant to close and make her way down to the harbour, but just to reassure herself that she was doing the right thing, she would call in at Heather's on the way down. As she got to the shop, Marco was in full swing with a customer – a rather large lady who was trying to buy a kaftan.

"No, you need something more fitted which will show off your curves. You have a wonderful figure. Don't hide it under that tent. Trust me, I know what I'm talking about." Eventually the lady agreed and thanked him.

"Hello, Carolina. Your turn for the Marco makeover. Something pink, I think."

"Thank you, Marco, but the only thing I need is some flat shoes and new knees. Can you do that?"

"Oh, don't be silly. You're too young for flat heels, my darling. Show off those fabulous legs."

After laughing with Marco and Heather's reassurance that she was doing the right thing, Carolina left and made her way down the hill to the restaurant.

Cleo was taking everything in and was about to settle her bill when Andréas came over with another gin and tonic. She explained that she hadn't ordered one, but Andréas said that it was from Nico and he hoped that he could join her for a drink once he had ended his phone call. Cleo agreed. She knew that her mother didn't like him, but she thought he was quite handsome and very charming. She was on holiday and perhaps it was time to have some fun. Nico was just about to join Cleo when Carolina walked in.

"Nico, can I have a word, please, if it's convenient?"

Nico knew he needed to stay on the right side of his aunt. Carolina explained the situation and Nico said that the reason for the cash flow problem was because of the changes he was making. He promised her that everything would be resolved next week. His new hip bar was about to launch. The furniture was arriving tomorrow and by this time next week the money would be rolling in. Carolina felt like exploding with anger, but it was none of her business. She was just doing the paperwork while her brother was in hospital.

"Okay thanks. I just thought I should mention it, but if you've got everything in hand. I'll get going."

"Thanks again for all your help, Carolina. Goodbye."

"Now, young lady. I think we need to start again. I don't think your mum approved of me. I'm Nico and you are?"

"I'm Cleo and I'm old enough to choose my own friends. I don't need my mother to do it for me. By the way, thanks for the drink."

Three hours later and the last sea taxi had departed on its final return trip to Volmos. The staff had finished clearing up and had left Cleo and Nico sitting and flirting with each other. She might have had far too many drinks, but she wasn't drunk enough to take him up on his offer to have another drink at his dad's house. Nico finally gave up trying. He might have lost this one, but there would be others. He walked Cleo back to the taxi rank and politely said goodnight as she made the return trip back to her mother's.

Cleo crept back in without Sarah hearing her. She

was excited, but slightly drunk and her head was buzzing. She knew she had to be careful and she needed to think through all her ideas properly.

The following morning Cleo got up early. She was on a mission, but for the time being it would have to be a secret mission.

"Morning, darling. You're up early. Did you have a nice evening? I didn't hear you come in."

"Yes, Mum, I had a lovely time. I caught a taxi back, not the sea one. What shall we do today? If I can suggest something, I'd really like to go and have a look at that shop where you bought all your fabulous new clothes. Is that alright?"

"Oh yes, but you must stop me from buying anything. If Marco is there, that will be difficult as he's so clever at persuading me to buy things. Thing is, I never regret it."

"I can't wait to meet this Marco. He sounds like fun."

Sarah and Cleo had breakfast and coffee and then Cleo showered and got herself ready. Sarah suggested they walk up so she could show Cleo the views from the foot of the castle. Just like everyone else, Cleo was impressed.

"I can quite see why you've fallen in love with this island, Mum, with its views, the people, the food and the way of life. I do think it's very special. It's beginning to perform its magic on me as well."

Sarah knew her daughter too well. What was she up to and who did she see last night?

Once at the shop. Marco was on top form. After kisses and introductions, he started talking about clothes, but to Sarah's surprise he didn't try to sell her anything. He explained that until new stock arrived, he thought she had everything in the shop that would suit her, but as for Cleo..."

"Now, my dear, what are you looking for? Glam evening outfits, comfy day wear or sexy, having fun clothes?"

"Well. I like these tops and with a baggy pair of cotton trousers I think that would look good on me."

"Oh no, you don't want to cover your legs with every day practical clothes. No, you need glam."

Cleo insisted on buying three pairs of trousers and five tops. Marco was more than pleased with the sale, but he really didn't think it was her style unless she was going to wear them for work. Sarah had her suspicions and if she was correct, her daughter was up to something. They said their goodbyes and decided to go for a drink and a bite to eat. Sarah said to herself that if Cleo wanted to tell her what she was up to, no doubt she would in her own time.

Down in the harbour Nico set about explaining his plans to the staff. Over the few weeks he had been there he had realised that it wouldn't be possible to do what he wanted without implementing many changes and causing upset. It was a very close community and he didn't want to cause any trouble. More than anything he needed Andréas to back him and so he waited for the busy lunch time trade to finish.

"So, Andréas, it's time to tell you my plans. Don't worry, it won't affect you. Your job is safe. I've decided to split the restaurant into two halves. One half will stay just the same as it is now although I'll try and squeeze in a few more tables in. You'll have the path into the inside but on the other half there'll be my chic new chill-out bar. The new furniture for that is on its way. There'll be a screen separating the two halves. Isn't it exciting? The money we lose by not having so many tables will be outweighed by all the cocktails and champagne we'll sell. No one will lose their jobs as we'll be taking so much money. Dad will see that the chill-out bar is making more money and then next season we'll reopen without the food part. How exciting it that?"

Andréas kept his mouth closed and smiled. At least

they were all going to keep their jobs. That had been his main concern.

"Oh, one more thing, Andréas. I've got a big surprise. A friend is coming to help me with the bar and I hope you will make them feel very welcome. I'm sure there was something else. Oh, yes. This is the difficult part. I need to find somewhere for Angelo to move to as I'm moving into the flat above the business when my dad gets back from Athens."

"So, Mum, what do you want to do now? Shall we take a walk into town?"

"Ohm I don't mind, Cleo, whatever you want. I'm up for a nice night out. I had so much sleep last night that I'm ready to party. How about you?"

Cleo realised that she needed to tread carefully. Her mother knew she was up to something.

"I think we should get some food and stay in for the evening. Is that alright?"

"Yes, that's fine with me. It's your holiday and we need to make the most of it. By the way, when did you say you were going home?"

Chapter 28

The following morning Cleo lay in bed wondering how to tell her mother that she would be staying. Living here wouldn't be the problem as Sarah would love having her daughter on the island, but the job was more of an issue. Actually, it wasn't the job itself, but more about Nico. Sarah wouldn't approve, but Cleo was now an adult and needed to persuade her mother that everything would be alright.

Up in Creakos, Andréas explained Nico's plans to Carolina. She felt a little better about the restaurant. At least there was not going to be any structural changes and everyone would be keeping their jobs. Among everyone she knew on the island, surely someone would be able to rent Angelo a room. They just needed to wait until Giorgio was out of hospital and back on the island.

It was still early and Cleo had come up with a solution. She was going to text her brother, Henry. She could rely on his support as he was always concerned for her welfare when she was out and about in London. At least here she was safe. Cleo waited for a reply from Henry, but it was time to get up and she need a way of getting to the restaurant without Sarah coming with her.

"Morning, darling. Did you sleep well? What would you like to do today?"

"Oh, I don't really mind. We could go to the beach if you like. Is that your phone I can hear, Mum?"

As Sarah answered her phone, Cleo texted Henry again. She didn't know why he hadn't replied to her. It was now half past nine and he should be up.

"Cleo, I've got some good news. That was your

brother on the phone. Guess what? He's flying over tomorrow. He didn't say how long for, but won't that be lovely? Both my children here at the same time. It will be a real holiday. I'm so happy. He said that from all the texts you've sent him describing the beautiful island, he felt that he was missing out. I don't know about the beach now. I think I need to organise a few things. You don't mind going by yourself, do you?"

Sarah began to make a list of things she needed to do, and Cleo got ready. Now she didn't need to make any excuses. She could just catch the sea taxi over to the harbour and see Nico. It was turning out to be a good day, and once Henry was here he would see Nico's restaurant was the perfect job for her.

"Right, I'm going to call in on Miriam and ask whether it's alright for Henry to stay. I'm sure it will be, but I had best check first. Shall we meet back here at around seven? Have a lovely day, darling, and remember to keep applying the sun lotion. The heat can be very deceiving when there's a sea breeze."

"Don't worry, and please don't go to too much trouble for me and Henry. See you later."

"Oh, do come in, Sarah. How are you? Do you have time for a coffee? Are you having a good time with your daughter?

'Yes, coffee would be lovely, thank you."

Miriam made the coffees and they went into the garden. Sarah explained about Henry coming to stay, what she and Cleo had been up to and she also mentioned how that creepy bloke Nico had tried to chat Cleo up but she had put a stop to it. When he was in the restaurant she had noticed that the atmosphere didn't seem the same. Miriam said that she knew all about it as Carolina had told her how she couldn't wait for her brother to come back as hopefully things would then return to normal.

"Now, tell me about your son. Is he bringing a girlfriend to stay with him? Do you need extra bedding and towels? Oh, Sarah, this is exactly what you need. I'm so pleased for you. After all that's happened, you're beginning to make a fresh start."

"Yes, I'm feeling good, Miriam. No, Henry doesn't have a girlfriend. He's always been too career minded, and to be honest he doesn't have many friends. After university he got a job researching geological things for the government. His work takes him all over the country, but the good thing is he can sometimes work from home. I have so much to thank him for as far as my charity work is concerned as he accompanies me to functions when his father is busy with other matters – or should that be when he's with his mistress. It will be nice to have both of them here with me."

Down in the harbour there was a hive of activity. Nico had arrived at the restaurant before any of the staff and had started rearranging the tables on what would be the food side. He had cleared the other side for all the new furniture which was arriving. When Andréas arrived, other restaurant owners kept walking by muttering about what Giorgio would have to say about it. However, that was only the half of it.

"So, Andréas. I've had a phone call. The van containing the new furniture is on the ferry in Preveza and will be here in less than two hours. You and Angelo carry on as normal and I'll deal with the delivery. By the way, later I need to tell Angelo that he has to move within two weeks."

Cleo was now ready and off to catch the sea taxi. She was excited as this was the start of a new adventure helping to run the new bar. By the time she arrived in the harbour, Andréas and Angelo were serving morning coffees and pastries and preparing for the lunch time trade. The restaurant looked strange with half of it empty.

"Morning, Nico. This is exciting. I thought I'd stop by and see when you wanted me to start."

"Hello, my lovely. Yes, it's very exciting. Well, the bar opens tomorrow night but there's an official launch on Saturday night. You can start today though. The area where I've moved all the chairs and tables away from, needs a thorough clean. One of the kitchen staff will show you where we keep the mops and buckets."

"You want me to clean? I thought you wanted me to help run it, not be your cleaner?"

"Oh, my darling, we all have to chip in and get things sorted over the next few days. Of course you'll be helping me. Have I told you how gorgeous you look today? I think we need to spend some time discussing the job, so how about we get together somewhere a bit quieter tonight and I run through everything? I need to make a few calls now, so you just get on with making the place look fresh and clean before the furniture arrives."

"Okay then. By the way, I've bought some lovely smart clothes, which will be perfect for running a bar. Nice cotton trousers and tops."

"Trousers, my darling? I'm not having a beautiful creature like you in trousers. Oh, no, it has to be miniskirts or tight little shorts and perhaps some vests. This is a fun bar. People want to feel like they're at a party, not going to the bank. Now if you get on with the cleaning, we can talk about making you sexy later."

Andréas smiled to himself. Oh dear, this poor girl will be working her socks off while Nico swans about chatting up all the guests. I wonder how long this will last. With that his phone rang. Carolina had phoned to say she had found Angelo a little room in a house on Volmos. He would have to share the bathroom and kitchen with three waiters from one of the hotels, but it would be a start until he found something better.

Cleo felt hot, sweaty and sticky. She had never done work like this before. Thank goodness it was just a one-off. Once the bar was open, she would be checking that the other staff were doing the cleaning properly. Nico was right about the clothes. It was a party bar and she needed to look like she was at the party. She had finished the cleaning and the furniture was being unloaded, so she said her goodbyes and planned to meet Nico at nine o'clock. Before heading back to Volmos, perhaps she should call up to see if Marco had anything more suitable for her to wear.

Despite it not being any of her business, Carolina felt she should warn Sarah about what Cleo was getting into with Nico. Andréas had told her that Nico was only after good looking girls who would attract young men into the bar and get them spending their money, so she decided to walk down to Volmos.

"Hello, how are you, Cleo? Is your Mum with you?"

"No, not today. The thing is, I need your help but at the moment it's a bit of a secret."

Cleo continued to explain the whole story about the job and needing to look sexy. Marco had been around long enough to realise that Nico was dangling her on a piece of string as all he was interested in was making money without doing any work himself. Cleo needed clothes and he would help her, but he would not be making her look tarty. Sexy is one thing, but cheap and tacky is another. Over the next hour Cleo tried on lots of lovely party looking outfits that were comfortable to work in. Job done!

Down on Volmos Sarah had invited Carolina in and over a glass of wine had delicately explained and reassured her that come the beginning of October when the town closes down and becomes quiet, Nico will be on his way. Sarah said that Cleo was old enough to make her own mistakes, but at least she would be there to help pick up the pieces.

"So you plan on staying here when it's cold and wet on Holkamos during the winter? Nothing happens then as only a few restaurants stay open."

"It can't be any worse than England with its ice, snow, wind and grey outlook. I don't know what life has in store. At some point I need to sort out a divorce but there's no rush. It's not as if I need it to get married again. The last thing on my mind is another relationship."

"Oh, perhaps that last sentence is one I should answer."

"What do you mean?"

"Well, you have an admirer who just happens to be moving from Holkamos town down here on to Volmos."

"Please tell me it's not Nico. He's far too young for me. Saying that, he's far too old for Cleo."

They both laughed and Carolina told Sarah all about Angelo and how he'd worked for the family for more than 30 years. To be honest, her father had always treated Angelo as part of the family as he didn't have a family himself.

Cleo was happy with her new clothes. They weren't the type of thing she would have normally worn, but this was Greece. It was the summer and it was time to have fun.

"Just one thing, Marco. Could I leave the clothes here for a few days just until I tell my mum about the job?"

"Of course, darling. I'll give you my mobile number and when you're ready, either Heather or myself will drop them down to you."

Cleo really couldn't put this off much longer. She needed to go back and tell her mum everything. For one thing, she needed to make an excuse to go out with Nico tonight.

*

The furniture was now unpacked. Andréas could see it was very modern and certainly not cheap, but it stood out like a sore thumb. The screens helped it to become two separate businesses, but it wasn't right for Holkamos. This was more like an Athens night club. Oh, dear. Just wait until Giorgio sees it.

"You're early, darling. I wasn't expecting you for a couple of hours. How was the beach? I'm all ready for Henry's visit."

"I've something to tell you, Mum. I don't want you to be angry, but I love being here with you, and as it's such a beautiful island I thought I may stay for a while, if that's alright. While I'm here I've decided to work, so I've got myself a little job in a bar. It's a management position and I thought it would be good experience for me. Please don't try and talk me out of it, Mum, as it won't work."

"Oh, darling, that's wonderful. I wouldn't dream of talking you out of it. How exciting for you, and a management position too. You're such a clever girl. I'm delighted for you. So, when do you start?"

"What, you don't mind? Oh, thanks so much, Mum. I start tomorrow, but I'm meeting the owner for some training tonight."

"Well, if that's what you want to do, and if they're good people to work for, treat you with respect and don't put on you, then I'm very happy."

Cleo was surprised at her mother's reaction but once she was in the shower thinking about it, she knew that nothing on the island would stay a secret for long and also that Sarah was quite astute. Somehow her mother knew exactly where and who she was going to work for. Good people, respect... Well, she thought to herself, I'm going to prove he's a lovely man who wants me not just to work with, but as a girlfriend too. I'll show you that

I'm old enough to make the right decisions.

Back in the restaurant at nine, and looking and feeling like a million dollars, Cleo was ready to prove to Sarah that she was an adult.

"Hello, darling. You're looking more gorgeous than ever. What do you think of the new furniture? It's hot, don't you think, just like you? Now, I planned to go through all the cocktails with you, but I've left the menus at my dad's. Why don't we pop over to his house and go over them there? It will give us a chance to get to know each other a little better."

Andréas wished he had made a list of how many girls had fallen for Nico's charms over the years. Sadly, there were too many to count, but this one was different. This was no ordinary holiday maker. This one was going to be working for him. The big question was how long for. Training was a new name for it, he thought to himself.

Giorgio's house was modest and simple rather than the glamorous home Cleo imagined. However, it was the son she was interested in, not the father.

"Before I show you the menus, I think I should make you one of the cocktails. My friend, the cocktail barman will be arriving tomorrow. You'll like him as he's fun. Do you know, Cleo, so many girls have asked for your job, but the minute I saw you I knew you were the one. I can tell we're going to make a great team. Now before I go through the menu, try this. It's good, don't you think?"

"It's very strong. I don't think it needs as much alcohol. I think it's gone straight to my head, perhaps because I've not eaten anything. How about we go for something to eat, a nice romantic meal."

"Perhaps later. Let me run through the job description. You'll stand by the entrance. When a few men walk by, it's your job to get them into the bar and recommend some cocktails. The more they drink, the better the tips."

Nico explained that he would focus on getting groups of girls in. By this time Cleo was on her third cocktail and couldn't really concentrate on anything Nico was saying.

"You know, Cleo, you're very special. I think the bar is going to be so much better with you on board."

With that Nico leaned over to kiss her, but the mixture of cocktails made Cleo sick.

"Oh, God. I think you'd best go and I'll clean this up. I'll see you tomorrow. Just walk down the street and you'll see the taxi rank. Oh, another thing. I think we should keep our relationship a purely business one, and then once the bar closes at night it will be our time."

The next thing Cleo could remember was waking up at home. It was morning and Sarah was out. Oh, God, what must Nico have thought of me, she wondered. I really showed myself up.

"Hello, darling. Welcome to Greece. This is Melvin, who I rent the house from. He's kindly driven me here to meet you. Did you have a good flight?"

Once in the car Melvin could sense an atmosphere. Was Henry not too happy about his mother being in Greece? At the end of the day she hadn't done anything wrong and it wasn't any of his business.

Down on Volmos, Cleo had showered and was feeling a lot better. She checked her phone and had seen that the plane had arrived, so it would only be another hour or so and they'd all be together. She knew it would feel strange, plus she needed to go to work. With that, her phone signalled a text message. It was Nico to see whether she was alright and also to say that the bar wouldn't be opening until the next day as the new cocktail manager couldn't get to Holkamos. That was good news. Cleo had an evening to convince Henry that life was good and to get him on side. She then phoned Marco to ask him to drop the clothes off at some point. Everything was good. She had a new job and a new boyfriend, although a bloody awful hangover.

Henry and Sarah arrived and they showed him around. He was very quiet which wasn't unusual, that was his normal behaviour. It took Sarah about three hours to persuade him to change his corduroy trousers for a pair of shorts and a T-shirt. This was a holiday after all.

"So what would you like to do? Shall we catch the sea taxi into Holkamos town?"

"Oh, no, Mum. There's plenty of time for Henry to see that. Let's have a quiet night here, a nice salad and some barbecued pork. You'd like that, wouldn't you, Henry?"

"Whatever suits you two. I haven't come here to upset your routine. Just carry on as normal."

"If you haven't come to upset our routine, darling, why have you come? Has your father sent you to check up on me? He obviously doesn't have the time to come himself as he's probably with his mistress, the woman he's been cheating with for, is it ten or fifteen years? Oh, it's more like twenty years. Come on, Cleo, you can come and help me carry the shopping. When we get back, hopefully your brother will have taken that look of distain off his face and be starting to enjoy himself."

Henry did feel guilty. He and his mother did have a lovely relationship, but it was his job to persuade her to come home and put everything behind her. He went and sat in the garden and as he was relaxing in the sunshine, he could hear something. Someone was calling.

"Hello, girls, are you decent? It's only me. Don't worry, I'm not trying to sell you anything. No need to cover your boobies. They're of no interest to me. Oh, sorry, who are you?"

"No, I'm the one who should be asking you that question. This is my mother's house."

"Oh well, it's not you I've come to see this time, but dearie, if you keep your fingers crossed and say a few prayers your time might come. To be honest, if anyone ever needed a Marco makeover it looks like it's you."

"My mum and sister are out. How I can help?"

"Oh, you might need a makeover, but I must say you're very forward, but not now as I've not got the time. Could you give your sister these bags? Thank you, and before I go, can I just say one thing? You're on holiday, so it wouldn't hurt to smile. Oh, and by the way, Marco does like a challenge. Goodbye, my lovely."

With that Marco left, but it did cross his mind that with a bit of thought and imagination he could probably make something out of Henry. Goodbye undertaker, hello human being.

By the time Sarah and Cleo returned Henry had tried to cheer up. Sarah had calmed down and they had a lovely evening. There was no mention of divorce or going home to England. Cleo was excited about her job and Henry wanted to know all about the island and its history.

"Oh, I forgot to tell you. While you were out shopping someone dropped some bags off for you, Cleo. I took them to my room, so I'll go and get them for you. By the way, he seemed a bit of a character, but a little scary. He reckoned he could do things for me. All very strange."

"Oh, that's Marco. He's reinventing both Mum and me. You could do with letting him give you the Marco makeover too."

Chapter 29

The following morning Cleo was up early. She was excited to be going off to her new job and decided to walk rather than catch the sea taxi. She wanted to stop off and thank Marco. She wasn't wearing any of her new clothes as that would look as though she was on her way home after a hard night partying. Henry and Sarah both wished her well and off she went. Sarah was determined to have a lovely day with Henry, but she knew she first needed to clear the air. Why was he here and what was he up to? The one thing she was sure of over the last few weeks was that she had been able to clear her head. Emotions had been put to one side and this was a new start for her. Perhaps not on this island, but somewhere where she could start again.

"Good morning, darling. How are you? Did you try on all the outfits again?"

"Hi, Marco. Thanks for dropping them off. Yes, one of them will get its first outing tonight when the new bar opens. I'm so excited and I just wanted to thank you for bringing them down to Volmos."

"That's okay. Good luck with the new job. I might pop down to see if there's any hot men around. Talking of hot men, I met your gorgeous brother yesterday. I say gorgeous because he would be if I got my hands on him and gave him the Marco makeover."

"Well, someone needs to get their hands on him. Looking like he does, he'll never get himself a partner."

"Excuse me. It could be a boyfriend."

"Oh, Marco. You're so funny."

Back on Volmos, Sarah made coffee and took it out into

the garden where Henry was checking emails on his phone. She waited until he finished and then set about clearing the air.

"So what's the problem, Henry. We've never kept secrets from each other. Unlike your sister who has hidden agendas, we've always talked about everything. I want us to have a nice time while you're here, but that won't happen until you spill the beans. Come on. Get it all off your chest and then we can go and have some fun."

"He says he's sorry and he wants you back. The last thing he wanted to do was upset you."

"That may be what he wants, but what about you, Henry? What do you want?"

"I want you both to be happy."

"We're not talking about a one-night stand here. He's had a mistress for many years. How do you think that makes me feel? I was good enough to run the hall and organise his life, but when it came to anything else, he went to her."

"But he says he's sorry."

"I can accept his apology, but it's time for me to move on. I can become bitter and twisted over all this or I can move on. You said you want me to be happy. I am happy, Henry. My beautiful children mean everything to me. Now my life consists of watching them grow up and enjoy their life. Your father made his choice and he chose her. Would you be happy if I went back to him and at every function and event we went to, people would be saying, 'Poor Sarah, you know what her husband did?' Is that what you want?"

They sat in silence for the next hour and eventually Sarah went to have a shower. Henny was her son and she loved him more than anything in the world, but he needed to understand the severity of his father's actions.

*

Down in the harbour the new barman had arrived. He was polishing glasses and setting up his station, but there was no sign of Nico. Cleo said good morning to Andréas and Angelo before going into the back of the bar to put her bag away.

"Hi, I'm Pete, the new barman."

"Hello, I'm Cleo, the assistant manager and Nico's girlfriend. Nice to meet you."

"Is Nico with you? I've not seen him so far today."

"No, I thought he'd already be here. I'm not sure what I should be doing."

"He left a note saying that I had to set the bar up and that when the girl comes to get her to wipe down the tables and dust the chairs. I suppose that means you."

Cleo was disappointed that Nico had referred to her as 'the girl' but he had said that they'd all have to muck in with the chores until everything was up and running smoothly. She wasn't sure about Pete. He was completely different to Nico. He came across as quite shy. That's neither here nor there, she thought, I'd best get on with the cleaning.

While Sarah was in the shower, there was a knock at the door. Henry answered it and discovered Miriam there, who introduced herself and explained that she wished to invite all three of them to dinner one night. Henry said he'd pass the message to Sarah and that she would get back to her.

"Was that someone at the door, darling?"

Henry explained the reason why Miriam had called and they both decided to go to the beach for the day with books. There was no mention of their earlier conversation. Henry knew he had to give things some thought. Secretly he knew how he felt about everything. His dad was in the wrong and his mother had been hurt. It was a black and white situation just like his work decisions were.

*

Cleo was out the back getting a fresh bucket of water when Nico arrived. Pete had noticed him planting a kiss on a girl's mouth just before he walked into the bar.

"Morning, matey. How's it going? You've done a fabulous job setting up all the bottles. Like I always said, if ever I was to open a bar, I'd only have the best cocktail barman for my business."

"Hi Nico, your girlfriend's out the back."

"My what? Oh, hi, darling. How are you today? Sorry, I'm late. I just had a bit of business to sort out. Come and give me a kiss before we get stuck in."

"Nico, Cleo and I have been stuck in, as you put it, for the last few hours. Can't you see that?"

After four hours of lying on the beach, Sarah suggested she and Henry either go for something to eat at one of the beach restaurants or catch the water taxi over to the harbour. Henry wanted to go back and have something in the garden, so on the way back they stopped off at the shop and bought some crusty bread and pate.

"Oh, just before we go in, I'll tell Miriam that we'll accept her offer for dinner later in the week. You go in and put the kettle on. Here, can you take the bag?"

Henry opened a packet of olives and prepared the bread and pate. Instead of making coffee he opened a bottle of wine and drank the first glass before Sarah returned. He realised where his loyalties had to lie, and the sooner they talked about it the better.

Andréas and Angelo struggled with the new layout of the restaurant. The tables had been pushed too closely together and people couldn't get pushchairs around them. This was affecting the money they were taking. They also needed to pass by with hot plates, and as they couldn't get behind the chairs this was becoming a big problem. A couple who had come in for a quiet lunch time drink found themselves having to put up with children banging their chairs. Something needed to be done about it. The bar side was all ready, sparkling, fresh and new. Nico called Pete and Cleo to pull up a chair so that they could all go through the plans for the night.

"First of all, thank you both for all you've done today. It's going to be such an exciting evening. However, I'm a little worried that a lot of the older people who live here will be curious and want to see what's going on. We will have to discourage them. We want the young, good looking clientele. This is the start of us transforming this sleepy, dull island into a party island, so lots of smiles. Like I said before, Cleo, the minute you see some good-looking blokes passing by, drag them in and sell them some drinks. Make them feel special. It's all about making them feel important and then they'll be back night after night. Are there any questions?"

"Yes, just one. Nico, when do the other staff arrive?"

Pete looked the other way and seemed embarrassed by Cleo's question. She wanted to meet them and get to know them before the bar opened.

"Oh, Cleo, darling, we are the staff. The three of us. It's just us."

"Oh, sorry. When you said I was going to help to run the place, I presumed there would be other staff. I'm sorry I've got confused. Just one more thing, who does the work on our days off?"

"Cleo, hasn't your boyfriend told you it's going to be us, seven days a week, until we shut for the winter? That's normally the first week of October, isn't it, Nico? I reckon we've got at least another fifty days of smiling ahead of us. Teeth and tits, Cleo, teeth and tits."

"Oh, Henry, that's lovely, and wine, thank you."

"I'm sorry, Mum, for not being myself these last few days. It's just that I thought that if you weren't home with us, you'd be unhappy. I can see it's the complete opposite though. You're so relaxed here, but it can't continue. At some point you'll have to go back to England and sort things out properly. You won't have to do it alone as I'll be there with you. Anyway, that's a long way off. We're on holiday and holidays are all about having fun."

"Thank you, darling. That means so much to me, but I don't want you to feel you have to take sides. I know what your father has done is wrong, but he'll always be your father and you need to have a good relationship with him."

"He didn't just cheat on you, Mum. He cheated on me and Cleo too. There were times when he should have been with us and he chose her. That's wrong, so very wrong, and I think that's where this conversation should end. We have something else to worry about now, and that's the mess my sister has got herself into."

"So it's not just me who's concerned about Cleo?"

"Oh no, were you in the mood for going to a cocktail bar? It has to be done and hopefully only the once."

"Right then, Marco. Are you ready for a staff night out?"

"What do you mean, Heather? I thought as it was Edelina's night here in the shop we could all doll ourselves up and go to the new cocktail bar, if you're up for that."

"Yes, that would be lovely, Heather, but just one thing. I have never and will never doll myself up. My creations are nothing more than perfect and a million miles away from dolling up."

It was seven o'clock and the harbour was turning from day to night. Andréas was dreading the evening trade, but like his mother had said he was going to keep quiet. How things would pan out, only time would tell. Cleo had changed clothes and put some make up on. Pete was wearing a silly shirt that Nico had got for him and they were ready to go. This was the opening of the new cocktail bar. Sadly, Pete and Cleo were not as excited as Nico but at least they were ready. Nico was right about lots of his father's friends wanting to come and see what was going on and as he didn't really want to upset them, he gave them free drinks and hoped they wouldn't stay for too long.

Sarah wanted Henry to experience that special moment when the sea taxi disappeared around the bottom of the cliff and you could see Holkamos harbour in the distance. She'd talked so much about it, but it really was a memory to last a lifetime.

"You were right, Mum. That's such a special view. I'm beginning to realise why you've fallen in love with this island."

Before going to the cocktail bar they decided to take a walk around and get something to eat. Sarah had suggested that Henry choose but he said that she knew all the best places. There was only one place, but as it was now half the size, they probably wouldn't be able to get a table. After a stroll around the streets, looking at all the crafts in the shops and taking in all the cooking smells from the restaurants, Sarah led the way to her favourite. It was empty apart from just a few tables of people as the screen was up and they couldn't see into the bar.

"Andréas, why is it so quiet?"

Sarah realised the reason was the music coming from the bar. It wasn't the type of music you'd want to listen to while eating, but as the food was good and she was fond of the place they decided to stay and put up with the loud pumping beat. After introducing Henry to Andréas and Angelo, Sarah started to recommend the different dishes she had enjoyed over the previous few weeks.

Next door in the bar area, Pete and Cleo were chatting as they didn't have any customers. Nico had said it was probably too early. Pete was telling Cleo that the reason he came was that he owed Nico a favour. They weren't good friends really. They just knew each other from years ago, and as Pete was going travelling around Australia, this was a chance to earn some money before he set off.

"So what are you going to be doing when this closes in October? Will you go back to England?"

"I've not given it any thought. Nico mentioned that because we'll be working hard over the next few months, once it closes we'll be able to have some fun."

"Talking of Nico, where's he disappeared to?"

"Oh, he said he was having a walk around the harbour to get some of the young people he knows to pop in."

Carolina, Katia and the children had come down from Creakos to have a look at the bar and on the way across the harbour front they bumped into Heather and Marco.

"Hi, Carolina. Those grandchildren of yours seem to grow by the day. Are you going to the new bar? I don't really think it's my thing, but I thought Marco deserved a night out."

"Oh, Heather, a night out indeed. I'm never in. Stop teasing me. If these young children weren't here, I'd be giving you a different answer."

They all laughed and headed for the bar where Cleo welcomed them in and showed them the cocktail list. Marco chose a rather flamboyant drink, but Heather, Katia and Carolina settled for a glass of wine each. They were just chatting when Sarah and Henry came in.

"Hello, Sarah. How are you? It's nice to see you again."

"Hi, this is my son, Henry."

"Oh, I've already met Henry, and I was right. You do need me to do a Marco makeover. Your beautiful stylish mother can't be seen out with someone looking like that."

Everyone giggled and even Henry saw the funny side of it.

"Now, Henry, you sit by me and I'll tell you about my plans to bring you into the twenty-first century."

With that Cleo emerged with the drinks. It was the first time Sarah had seen her in the new outfits and one look at Henry said it all.

"Hi, Mum. Hi, Henry. Welcome to the cocktail bar. What can I get you to drink?"

"Hello, darling. Just some wine for me, please."

"And the same for me, please, Cleo."

"Oh, Henry, you're so boring. It's a cocktail bar. Cleo, get your brother a drink like mine. It's called 'Sex on the Rocks'."

Everyone laughed, and with that Nico arrived back with a few friends. Carolina could see that it was the scrounging friend that he hangs around with in the restaurant, so there would be no money going in the till. As the evening progressed, it became busier and people were trying the cocktails, but Carolina noticed they only had the one drink. Had it still been the restaurant, they would be ordering bottles of wine and pints of beer. The more they had to eat, the more they would drink too. She thought to herself that the sooner Giorgio got better and returned from Athens, the sooner the place could return to normal.

Peter realised that Nico was playing on Cleo's emotions. He didn't have any interest in her apart from her working like crazy for him, but she was an adult and it wasn't his place to point it out to her. He also noticed that Nico was paying a lot of attention to three Greek girls who were on their fourth cocktail each. No money had gone into the till yet, but again that wasn't any of his business either. As long as he got paid and made a few tips for himself... that was the only reason he was there.

Carolina, Heather and the others had a really good evening. After several cocktails even Henry was laughing and enjoying himself. At one point he half agreed to a Marco makeover. They all left the restaurant together when it closed for the night. Andréas and the staff weren't happy because it hadn't been very busy and they hadn't received any tips. Everyone said their goodbyes, Cleo started to clear the tables and Pete was washing the glasses. His comment about there only being the three of them was wrong. The three had become two as Nico hadn't lifted a finger to help. Cleo said that she had noticed this but Nico had told her that if he was sitting chatting, it was to drum up more business. She then noticed that two of the Greek girls had left, but Nico was taking drinks over to the one girl who remained.

"Thank you both so much. I really appreciate how hard you've worked. Why don't you both go and I'll lock up. We can do it all again tomorrow."

"But Nico, I thought we were going to get something to eat when we finished. I thought I was..."

"Oh, darling, we're all tired. Perhaps tomorrow. There you go, see you later."

Pete felt sorry for Cleo, but that was Nico's nature. He needed someone pretty to sell the cocktails and that's what he had found in Cleo. Pete said he would walk to the taxi rank as the sea taxi had ended for the night and they said their goodnights to Nico and the Greek girl. So much for a lively party bar, but saying that, as no one was ordering cocktails, it had been an easy night for Pete pouring pints and uncorking bottles of wine.

Back on Volmos Sarah and Henry had gone to bed. Cleo

felt rather sad. She had worked so hard all day and all she wanted to do was to sit down with Nico and unwind. Saying that, he had such a lot on his mind with a new business and his father being ill, so it was understandable that he didn't have a lot of time for her. Once the holiday season was over they had the winter to look forward to together.

Chapter 30

Over the next few days everything continued in much the same way with Nico nowhere to be seen. The bar area was rather hit and miss. Sometimes it was full of people enjoying a cocktail, but then there would just be a few of the older local people being nosey and ordering coffee. Cleo did miss Nico's attention, although when he complimented her on how she looked, she smiled at him and thought that he did care for her. However, she was enjoying listening to Pete talking about his adventure to Australia. He had been planning this for years and the nearer it got to leaving, the more excited he was becoming.

Sarah and Henry either spent their days on the beach or in the garden. They had shared a few meals with Miriam and Melvin, and Henry had also phoned his father to tell him that there was no chance of talking Sarah into returning to the hall. This news hadn't gone down well, but he only had himself to blame. Today, however, there was no lying in the sunshine as they were both going out for the day. They were up early to meet Marco in the harbour for a short trip to Corfu. Sarah was excited, but Henry was slightly nervous. Today he would be getting the Marco makeover. Heather would also be with them as she had some jewellery to take to one of her suppliers.

On arrival at Corfu they went to the most fabulous bakery in the town which served the loveliest pastries and strongest coffee you could imagine.

"We've sat here long enough. We need to start working."

"What do you mean? We're only buying a few shirts

and shorts. You can't possibly call that work, can you?"

"Oh dear, Henry. I don't think you realise how serious this is. Did you want to come with me to deliver the jewellery, Sarah. I get the feeling the makeover could get a bit stressful."

"Stressful? I don't know what you mean. As long as Henry does as he's told, everything will be fine."

They all laughed, but strangely Henry looked a bit nervous again. So they wouldn't have to hang around waiting for each other, they decided to make their own way back to Holkamos. There were three boats later in the afternoon and early evening.

"Have fun, you two, but somehow I think we'll have more fun, don't you, Sarah?"

"All I'll say is take one last look at your son, Sarah. The next time you see him you won't recognise him."

They all went their separate ways and to Henry's surprise he found himself enjoying the afternoon. He'd never been clothes shopping with anyone before. Normally he only bought things which his father would have worn, like tweeds and corduroys. Marco liked to stop in different bars and restaurants to have a coffee here and a glass of wine there, and so the day was turning out to be such fun. Although Marco was very loud and flamboyant, deep down Henry realised that once there was no audience to perform to, he was actually rather shy and sensitive.

Back at the docks and with no sign of the other two, Sarah and Heather caught the boat home. They had also had a nice day and Sarah loved beginning to fit in with her new friends. She could be herself, the self she had never been before. As much as she missed all her charity work, surely it was now time for her. She did understand that there were things to resolve back in England, but she'd gone into the marriage with nothing and was prepared to leave with nothing. If he wanted a mistress, let him have one.

A few hours later and in the taxi with loads of bags and both a bit giggly from the wine, Henry and Marco were tired from all the walking and joked about some of the things Marco had made Henry try on. He hadn't let Henry buy anything that didn't suit him though as this was serious business rather than just fun. They paid the taxi driver and both with handfuls of bags headed over to get the boat back. They then realised that the last one back was seven o'clock. Marco had thought it was eight and so they had to phone Sarah and explain that they wouldn't be back until tomorrow.

Marco and Henry decided to go back to the town, find somewhere to stay and get something to eat. There was a little hotel with a few vacant rooms on one of the back streets and one was a twin room. A lovely lady showed them around the hotel. Once settled, they opened the complementary bottle of wine and lay on their beds.

"Can you be bothered to go out again, Henry? I'm not really hungry. Why don't we have an early night and then get the first boat back to Holkamos in the morning?"

"Yes, that's fine with me, Marco. If we're not going out, why don't you come over on to my bed and let me thank you for a lovely day. Somehow I think it isn't over yet."

Chapter 31

It was the first morning Sarah had found herself alone since Cleo and Henry's arrival and so she was up early. Henry was still in Corfu with Marco, and Cleo had left a note to say that she was going to the cash and carry in Preveza with Andréas. Nico had given her a list of things to get for the bar and Andréas needed some things for the restaurant. Sarah was enjoying having some time to herself, she needed time to think. Top of her list was Melvin and Miriam who were going to be locking the house up for the winter. In the second week of October they would be going back to England for a few months and Sarah needed to think about her plans for this time. Where would she go next?

"You've got your list then, Cleo, so let's hit the road. How are you enjoying being on Holkamos, and more importantly, how are you enjoying the job?"

"I love the island, the beaches and the people. I know the situation with my mum coming here was a bit odd, but I'm happy she chose this island. Have you lived here all your life?"

"Yes, although I nearly made a mistake and almost left once. Thankfully I didn't though. I'm really happy here. I have a lovely family and a good job, and I don't want to ever leave."

"Can I ask you something, Andréas? Why doesn't anyone in the restaurant like Nico? I get the impression that everyone loves his father, but when it comes to him it's a totally different matter."

"I don't think it's that people don't like him. It's just that Giorgio has worked hard all his life and people think Nico should help out more now his father isn't well. Nico just swans in for a couple of months and then goes again, normally leaving some trouble behind or a girl in tears. Sorry, perhaps I shouldn't have said that."

"That's alright. You haven't said anything I haven't heard before, but I suppose I'll have to go with my gut instinct. I believe he'll have more time for me once the holiday season's over. I'm sure he will."

"Yes, you could be right, Cleo. I shouldn't have said anything. Sorry."

"Good morning. Whoever would have thought that clothes shopping would turn into this. Next you'll be saying it's all part of the Marco makeover. Well, if that's so, I'm very happy. I think I know the best way to start the day off, don't you?"

Neither of them were really surprised about how the shopping trip had turned out. Right from that very first day when Marco had brought over Cleo's clothes to Volmos, there had been a spark between him and Henry, but sadly they needed to get back on the boat to Holkamos. Another half an hour wouldn't really matter, would it?

It was nearly lunch time and Sarah was contemplating what to do for the rest of the day when there was a knock on the door. That's nice, she thought to herself. That'll be Miriam. We'll be able to have a good chat and some coffee.

"Hello, Sarah. I thought that seeing as my wife, daughter and son were here, I might as well be here too. Can I come in?"

This was the last thing Sarah needed and she wished that either Cleo or Henry had been there to help break the ice. However, she was on home ground rather than being at the hall and so she led Philip into the garden and went to make them both a drink. She made two coffees and stopped to check her appearance in the mirror. Why, she didn't know, as most of the time she'd been on the island she hadn't cared less what she looked like.

"So, what brings you here, Philip? If it's the children, Cleo's at work and Henry's gone to Corfu with a friend."

"You know why I'm here, Sarah. It's to see you. We have things to sort out. We're still married and have commitments and responsibilities to other people."

Sarah hadn't given thought to the diary of commitments. She had sorted out all her charity meetings and events by emails but as far as hosting business dinners and events involving Philip was concerned, it had all hardly crossed her mind. Suddenly she thought, Oh, of course. He must be in a right state.

"So, what do you want to discuss?"

"Us of course. When are you coming home and why are the children here? How long is this holiday going to continue?"

"Philip, the 'children' as you put it, have been young adults for quite some time now and have come and gone, doing their own thing. I didn't ask or invite them to come here. Cleo has got herself a stupid job she'll be bored with within a few weeks, so she'll probably go back to London. Henry, I think, was curious to see what I was doing. Before long he'll be back in his office at the hall and I've got this place until October. Really, I think I should be asking you what your plans are."

"I made a huge mistake and I'm really, really sorry. It's over with her and I can't believe she went to the Press after all I'd done for her."

"Can you hear yourself? You're the one to blame, not her. Can't you see that?"

"What do you mean?"

"We could sit here discussing this for ages, but that won't resolve anything. I'll make us some lunch and then put a plan together. That's what I do, I've been planning everything for years."

Philip thought the conversation had gone better than he'd anticipated. He'd been expecting there to be shouting or even tears, but no, they were going to plan the future together. I've said sorry, and Sarah has forgiven me, he thought.

As Sarah prepared a few sandwiches she couldn't believe how calm she was. She shouldn't really have been surprised as calm could have been her middle name. She opened a bottle of wine and carried the tray into the garden, but before either of them could speak, the door opened and out came Cleo.

"Hello, darling. We have a visitor, and why are you back so early?"

"I don't need to be back at the bar until six-thirty. Dad! What are you doing here? Please tell me you haven't brought that woman with you."

"Now that's enough, Cleo. Calm down and give your father a chance to answer."

"Thank you, Sarah. It's lovely to see you, Cleo. Your mother says you've got a job here. That's nice. How are you enjoying it?"

"Yes, I have. My boyfriend's opened a cocktail bar and I'm helping him to run it, so I doubt I'll be going back to England for a while. Nico's ten years older than me, but by the way you've been carrying on behind Mum's back I don't think you're in any position to criticise me."

Before Philip had the chance to reply, the door opened again and in walked Henry.

"Hello, darling. Did you have a nice time in Corfu? Your father's here, and Cleo's just been telling him about her exciting news with the job and Nico."

"Hello, son. Seeing that you haven't answered any of my emails or returned any of my calls, I thought I'd better come and sort things out myself. You're obviously too busy visiting other islands."

"Sorry for any inconvenience, Father, but if you just

stopped to think, you'd realise that all this was brought on by you. If you hadn't done what you did, Mum would still be at home working her fingers to the bone organising your life for you and Cleo wouldn't be making a fool of herself with a lazy bar owner. However, I will say that thanks to you, I've just had one of the happiest days of my life. What else is there to say? Oh, yes, I'm gay and I've found myself a new boyfriend. His name is Marco."

With that, Cleo went off to her room and Henry made a coffee and went off for a shower, leaving Sarah and Philip to sit there in silence.

"But you two are like chalk and cheese, Marco. He's sort of frumpy and you're flamboyant. I don't understand that."

"Heather darling, that's why it works. We're complete opposites and excuse me, but he's far from frumpy now he's had the Marco makeover."

"Yes, but you're fun and like to be out partying, having excitement in your life. I think Henry would sooner be sitting at home reading a book."

"Well, my dear Heather, without going into details, the last thing on Henry's mind last night and first thing this morning, was reading a book. I won't say any more."

Pete had packed away the things that Andréas had left for the bar and was ready to go. Sadly, as it was midday no one wanted any cocktails, but it gave him time to plan his trip to Australia. He could hardly wait. After years in the planning, it would soon be happening and Pete was so excited.

"Hi, it's Pete. Sorry I've not really introduced myself. I'm Carolina, Andréas' mum and Nico's aunt. Is he around?"

"No, I'm afraid he isn't. He said that he wasn't going to come in until tonight. Can I help you?"

"No, don't worry. It's fine. I've come to collect the paperwork for the business. I'm doing it for my brother while he's in hospital."

"Oh, good luck with that. I've got the invoices for the goods Andréas got in Preveza today and here's the book with the money we've taken, if that's any help. Sorry, there's no money as Nico paid Cleo and myself our wages out of the takings."

"Thank you, Pete. That's a big help. By the way, if there's ever a problem with your wages, just let me know and I'll sort it out."

"So, our son is gay and our daughter's seeing an older man. Is there anything you want to tell me about your life too?"

"Philip, don't make me laugh. This whole situation has been turned around to suit you. It's not about your mistake any more. It's all mine and the children's fault. Do you know, if you'd had a one-night stand or a short affair, I might have forgiven you, but no, this has been going on for years. You were living a double life, one with us in the country and one in London for three nights a week. Can't you see how that makes me feel? I was more of a business partner and she was the wife. Yes, Philip, that's how it is. She may have gone now, but can you blame her? I expect you made her lots of promises you failed to keep and to be honest I think you probably got into something so deep you couldn't get out of it. This beautiful island isn't the right place to sort out our marriage. I'm happy to come back to England to go over all the details, but surely you can see it's over. We both have to move on with our lives. The children don't need us, and sadly I don't need you."

"I know it's been a bit of a shock me just turning up like this, but I'm going to be here for three days, Sarah. Perhaps you'll feel differently tomorrow and will talk about it. Here's a note of where I'm staying."

With that Philip left and Henry and Cleo emerged from their rooms. Henry cuddled Sarah and gave her a kiss. The children were both so proud to see how Sarah had handled the situation. She could easily have become emotional, but she had stayed calm, pointing out the facts. They loved their mother for this more than ever.

"So, excuse me, but is there no reaction from either of you to my news?"

"What news is that, Henry?"

"That I've come out, and said that I'm gay."

"Oh, darling. I've been aware of that since you were a teenager."

"Yes, and I've known it since you played with my dolls more than I did."

"We're both so happy for you, and as long as you have Marco in your life, we'll be the most stylish women around here. Isn't that right, Cleo?"

Chapter 32

Being brave in front of Philip was one thing but thinking about what to do next was quite another. Sarah was up early as she hadn't slept very well. Cleo was still asleep and Henry had stayed at Marco's. One thing Sarah was certain about was that at some point during the day she would be seeing Philip.

"Good morning, darling. You go and sit outside and I'll make us a coffee. How was your shift last night? You were very late coming home."

"Oh, it was really busy. A few yachts had come into the harbour with some spoilt rich kids in their twenties. They were the perfect customers for the bar, drinking all night but they were so rude shouting and clicking their fingers. They were so demanding that Pete and I didn't stop all night."

"Wasn't Nico there to help?"

"Well, yes, he did arrive as usual but very late. Apparently, he had a business meeting. Mum, did you know that everyone's telling me I'm a fool for putting up with his behaviour and he's just using me."

"Well, there's nothing to keep you there, so why don't you leave?"

"This might sound stupid, but I do enjoy the job. Pete and I get on really well and when he's not chatting about his big Australian adventure, we do have a laugh together. Those twits last night were a bit of a nuisance but they did leave us both with a fifty-Euro tip which I'll be taking up to my future brother-in-law to see what goodies he has on offer."

"I'm really happy for Henry. He's a bit like me in that all he ever does with his life is work. When I was young I had ambitions and I did fulfil them, but sadly on the way I did miss out on having fun. My darling, if you want to go and have a good time with Nico once the summer is over, you have my blessing."

"I'm not daft, Mum. Somehow, I think that when the season finishes, that will be the last I see of Nico. He wanted someone to work his bar so that he could enjoy the summer here on Holkamos."

"I'm glad you've realised that for yourself, darling. The cards are in yours and Pete's hands, as he needs both of you."

"Yes, he does, and I think it could be time for Mr Nico to have a taste of his own medicine."

"Henry, let go. I have to get ready for work. Heather and Edelina are expecting me in less than an hour."

"Just one more cuddle. I still need to thank you for the makeover."

"You must have a bad memory as you keep thanking me for that, not that I'm complaining."

Sarah phoned Philip and planned to meet him down on Volmos, suggesting they go for a walk up to Creakos. Philip seemed to be alright with this, but Sarah gained the impression from his tone of voice that he was ready for the worst. Cleo had left for work and there was a knock at the door. Miriam was standing there with some tomatoes from Melvin's vegetable patch. Sarah told her about Philip's arrival and that she was going to spend the day with him. Miriam wished her well and said that if she needed anything, all she had to do was ask.

"Sarah, it may be none of my business, but can I just say one thing? Some people do things wrong and get found out, while others never do. Life is both very complicated and strange. There are no set rules. What works for one couple, doesn't work for everyone, so you do need to follow your heart."

*

"Good morning, Cleo. How are you today? Yet again, we're the only two members of staff here."

"Hi, Pete. I'm fine. To be honest, I'm more than fine. I was thinking it's about time we had some fun in this bar and perhaps that might be at the expense of the missing member of staff. If we've very clever he won't even know it's happening. Are you up for it?"

With that, the young Greek girl who had been with Nico a few nights previously, came up to the bar and asked Pete whether Nico was around. Before Pete had time to answer, Cleo interrupted.

"Hi, no, he's not here until later tonight. He's had to take his wife for some scans as it's only a few weeks until the baby will be born. To look at him, you'd never guess that this will be Nico's fifth baby. Can I give him a message?"

With that the girl turned and ran away in tears.

"Fun, Pete. Yes, that's what the rest of the summer's going to be about. I might be blonde, I might be pretty, but I'm certainly not stupid."

Both of them stood there and laughed. This was going to be a summer they would never forget. As they were setting up the bar, Andréas popped his head around the screen wanting to know what all the amusement was about. When they told him what Cleo had just said to the Greek girl, Andréas joined in too.

"I'm glad you've seen through him, Cleo. You're a nice girl and it was upsetting seeing you being used. You weren't the first, and you won't be the last."

"Yes, but for the rest of the summer I'm on a mission to protect every young lady from his clutches. You watch me."

"Oh, by the way, Angelo's moving out of the restaurant today, so I'm by myself. Nico's promised to come and give me a hand, so I'm sorry to say that he'll be around all day."

"Melvin, I've made a coffee. Stop deadheading those cosmos and come over and chat to me."

"Come over and chat? That can only mean one thing, Miriam. You want to tell me what's on your mind."

"I was thinking that Sarah's husband was no worse than we were. He cheated, but so did we. His was a secret and so was ours."

"Oh, shut up, Miriam. Philip led a double life for many years. We had one little secret and I'm telling you that if it hadn't been for that, we might never have had these very special years together. If you continue talking like this I'll get up and continue chatting to the cosmos."

Sarah didn't want Philip coming to the house again and had arranged to meet him at the end of the lane. As she was waiting for him, she saw Angelo unpacking a van. They stopped to chat and he explained that he was moving into one of the houses. Sarah liked Angelo, but more than that she loved his simplistic lifestyle, free from worry. He lived on a beautiful island, doing a job he loved and was content. Is this the lifestyle she would want?

It was a bit of a cloudy day and the restaurant was getting busy during the lunch period. As Andréas had suspected, Nico was nowhere to be seen, but fortunately both Pete and Cleo helped out. They had a laugh and received some good tips, which was more money for Pete to take to Australia and for Cleo to buy clothes. At one point the restaurant became so busy that they removed a couple of the screens and set up the bar tables. Pete was a bit concerned about what Nico would say, but Andréas reassured him that it would be fine as it would be bringing money into the till.

Philip had arrived, and so Sarah said goodbye to Angelo and they went for their walk up to Creakos. Sarah told Philip how Cleo had finally seen through Nico and that she would probably return to England at the end of the holiday season. As for Henry, it had only been a question of time before he came out anyway.

"So, Sarah, that just leaves us. What do we do next? You can't stay here forever. I realise you don't want me anymore, and I can see why, but we do have responsibilities to other people, work charities and the estate. What happens to all of that?"

"I realise that, and I'll come back to the hall to sort things out in a few weeks' time. I want to see the summer out here with Cleo and I expect that Henry will work from here as Marco has to work until October. This takes me back to when they were younger and I had them around for the school summer holidays. I miss those times."

"Yes, you miss them, but I missed them altogether as I was never around. I really have messed everything up, but life could have been so different. We had such fun in the beginning. Can you remember the day I made such a fool of myself? I didn't have a clue what I was doing?"

"What was it you said? Oh, yes, I remember. You needed to book a private lunch for twelve. Three of the men were politicians from different political parties, but you failed to tell any of them that the others would be there. I went through the table plan you'd scribbled on a piece of paper two minutes before it was due to start and I pointed out that one of the MPs had gone off with the wife of the other. If it had all gone ahead, the invited Press would have had a field day."

"And from that day to now you've been sorting my life out for me. Oh, Sarah, you do deserve better than me, you really do. I've let you and the children down so badly. I could keep on saying, sorry, but I know that will never be enough."

"Right, come on. Let's drop all that for now and enjoy this beautiful island. When we get to the top, you can buy me a drink. Best foot forward."

"I don't think I've ever had a best foot. Most of my life I have been putting both feet in it."

Nico turned up at nine in the evening. The day had been so busy, but he came out with excuse after excuse which no one took any notice of.

"I'm sorry, Cleo. I promise I'll make it up to you. By the way, you know those three Greek girls I was talking to the other night? Well, I've just seen them in the street and they've had a right go at me shouting about how I don't deserve a good wife. I couldn't make head or tail of what they were talking about."

It got to eleven o'clock and Andréas hadn't stopped working all day. He and all the staff were starving hungry. The chef had cooked a moussaka and as they pulled together a few tables and poured some beers, Cleo asked if there was enough for another two.

"Pete, come on, the food's ready. It's time to eat. Nico's here now so he can manage. The shift's over. We haven't stopped for thirteen hours."

"Oh, Cleo, would it be alright if you took turns to eat. One helps me and then you swap around?"

"No, Nico, that wouldn't be alright at all. We're both exhausted. By the way, those tables need clearing. The people have just left and there's a group of eight coming for coffee at eleven-thirty. You do know how to use the coffee machine, don't you?"

Andréas could not wait to tell his Carolina and Katia all about it.

"Do you know, I was dreading the last few weeks of the summer but now I'm really looking forward to it. I can see Cleo will have Nico jumping through hoops."

*

As it was only midnight Pete and Cleo decided to go for a drink. As they were walking up towards the castle they bumped into Henry and Marco.

"Oh hello. We're off for a nightcap. Fancy joining us? It's like double dating."

"Yes, Marco, we'll join you but Pete and I aren't out on a date. We're just workmates going for a drink after work."

"Oh, I've heard that before. Come on, there's a lovely bar overlooking the castle. It's so romantic, so you never know, you might end up on a date after all."

Sarah was sitting in the garden reflecting on her day with Philip. Once they'd stopped talking about the future she had enjoyed herself. It had been just like going back to when they first met and went on holidays together. Sarah realised that she was her own worst enemy though. She couldn't remember a time when she wasn't organising Philip. He was useless, but to be honest, that was the thing that had attracted her to him in the first place.

Chapter 33

The following morning Philip returned to England. The future wasn't clear and over the next few weeks Sarah didn't have much contact with him. She sent him a text from time to time, but she was really happy, enjoying her summer. It was a special time spent with Cleo and seeing Henry so happy with Marco. There was never a dull moment when he was around! Her morning coffee with Miriam had become a regular thing and when Carolina joined them, it turned into lunch and sometimes even dinner. Sarah was beginning to feel more like a local than a holiday maker. Perhaps the island was becoming her home.

Andréas, Angelo and Pete didn't know what the day would have in store for them as that depended on how Nico had upset Cleo. The lazier and more annoying he was, the more Cleo wanted her revenge. A nice German girl had caught Nico's eye. She had been coming in with her friends for about four nights and as usual Nico hadn't charged them for their drinks. Pete had noticed this and that one night Nico had also gone to more trouble with his appearance. He overheard the girl saying to her friends that she would meet up with them in the morning. This meant one thing, she was going to go back to Nico's for the night. Pete told Cleo this and waited to see what she would do. When Nico went to the toilet, this was Cleo's opportunity to have some fun.

"Oh, hello, you don't mind if I sit here for a bit, do you? I've been on my feet all day, and to be honest, in my condition I should be resting. The doctor said I shouldn't be working more than five hours a day. It's my blood pressure. My mum was the same when she was pregnant with me."

"Oh, congratulations. You're having a baby. How exciting!"

"Thank you. Yes, it's very exciting, but I'm nervous as it's my first. Nico's excited about it too and he has so many plans. Of course, he hopes the first one's a boy."

"The Nico who owns this bar is the father?"

"Yes, the chap who's been bringing you the drinks."

With that, the girl got up and left. By the time Nico returned, Cleo was talking to the other customers and Pete was making cocktails.

"Pete, just a minute. Have you seen the girl I was talking to?"

"I think she just got up and left. Why?"

"No reason. I'm just a little confused. That's all."

On another occasion, Cleo had told an Italian gentleman that Nico was gay but very shy. This chap came in every night for a week and Nico couldn't get away from him. The biggest laugh they all had though was when a friend of Marco's, a drag artist from Athens, was staying on the island for the weekend. Cleo and Marco persuaded him to dress up as his drag persona, Mona, and try to chat Nico up. He had toned down his clothes and make-up and looked like a very glamorous model. All the restaurant staff were also in on the joke and all evening couldn't wait for Mona to arrive.

Henry, Marco and Mona first decided to have a meal in the restaurant, and as they sat eating and drinking, Mona caught Nico's eye. At first, he didn't know what to make of it. He said to Pete that the girl was rather unusual. Something about her was different, almost too perfect. Once they had finished eating, they moved next door to the bar and that's when the fun really started. Mona had a few drinks, knew everyone was watching and that it was time to perform.

Cleo ignored them and let Nico take the drinks order. Mona started flirting and his hand just happened to touch Nico's leg. As he passed by to go to the toilet, he put his hands on Nico's waist. None of them could keep a straight face, but Nico had taken the bait. There was only one thing on his mind. As the evening progressed, the flirting continued. The free drinks were flowing and everyone was waiting for the finale. The bar was nearly empty, Cleo and Pete were cleaning up and as usual, Nico was watching them. They couldn't remember the last time he'd helped them with anything.

"Come on, Mona. Let's go in for the kill. It's time to put him out of his misery."

Mona went to the toilet and on the way Nico asked whether she would like another drink or even go elsewhere for a nightcap.

"Oh, that would be nice. There's nothing more I like to do than share a night cap with someone. First I'll just go the toilet and say good night to my friends. Oh, one thing I should tell you, but I'm sure it won't be a problem, is that I'm a bit different. There's more to me than most girls."

"I know, you're special. This island doesn't get many girls as beautiful as you visiting it."

Mona seemed to be spending a long while in the toilet. In the meantime, Nico asked Pete to lock up. Everyone held their breath and then it happened. Out walked Mona minus the wig, make-up and clothes. There he was wearing jeans, shirt and a huge smile.

"Hi, Nico. I'm ready. Come and show me your night cap."

Nico was confused until he spotted the wig in one of Mona's hands and the stilettos in the other. He also noticed everyone looking and laughing at him. He turned to walk out.

"Nico, wait for me. We can still have a good time. I'll put the wig back on, if you like."

Everyone just roared with laughter. This had to be the best evening of the whole summer.

*

As it got to the middle of September, the atmosphere on Holkamos began to change, the families had left and it was starting to become a couple's island. The evenings were cooler, the cocktail bar just seemed to be selling coffees and brandies at night, but the restaurant was still as busy. Andréas had removed the screens so that they could use the bar tables to serve food. Pete and Cleo had become part of the restaurant team. After work they all socialised together and were just like a little family. There were days when Nico didn't even show his face, which was something they were all happy about.

September was always a good month at Edelina's. They all worked hard at selling their stock so that next year they could get lots of new ranges in. Marco was excited about going to choose the new clothes with Edelina, but he also realised that summer would soon be coming to an end and so would his summer romance. He and Henry hadn't discussed their future. Did they even have a future together? Heather was beginning to worry about Marco. She didn't want him to get hurt. Although he appeared to be loud and flamboyant, she knew it was a bit of an act and that secretly he was shy and insecure. Heather suggested Marco had three days off work and that perhaps he and Henry should go somewhere nice and have some fun. Marco agreed and the pair of them decided to take the boat over to the little hotel in Corfu where they'd stayed a few months back.

In Creakos, Carolina had heard from Giorgio. He was coming back to the island, but instead of going to his own house in the harbour, he wanted to stay with her for a few days. He didn't want anyone to know he was back, not even Nico. Carolina was pleased about this as it would give her time to slowly bring the news about the takings into the conversation. Not only was she worried about the takings, she was also concerned about the money that Nico was spending, and she also knew that Giorgio would blame everyone else. In his eyes, his son could do no wrong.

Getting off the boat in Corfu, Marco and Henry made their way to the hotel and dropped off their bags. Neither of them were in the mood for a stroll around the shops, so Henry suggested they hire a scooter and explore the island. Marco was up for this as they would be able to get away from all the tourist beaches and towns. It would be fun. They would then return to the buzz of Corfu town at night to eat and it would give them time talk about their future.

Sarah also needed to think about her future plans. The summer had been lovely, but all good things must come to an end. Over the previous few days she had been busy replying to emails from the various charities she worked with. They needed to book meetings and dinners, but most importantly they all relied on the ball as a massive draw to raise money. Having Lord and Lady Ferngate inviting you to events was always the icing on the cake, and as they were all aware of Sarah's circumstances, everything was up in the air.

"This looks like a nice place. Do you fancy eating here, Marco?"

"Yes, but do you think we could sit in the corner, out of the way?"

"You in a corner? That's a first."

They had a lovely meal and each consumed a fair quantity of wine. It was nice to be alone together, away from everyone else.

"So, Henry, what happens next? The summer's nearly over? Are you going back to England and will you come back to Greece one day?"

"I've got a very busy few months ahead. Apart from working, I've got to sort out somewhere to live. My father's given me permission to take over a couple of bedrooms at the hall and to turn one into a living room with a kitchenette. So although I'll be living in the hall, I'll have a small self-contained apartment in it. I just need to find someone with flair and style to design it for me. I don't really know how I want it to look, to be honest. It's very dated so it will need quite a big makeover to bring it into the twenty-first century. You have a busy time ahead too, what with going off and buying next year's stock for the shop."

"That will only take about three days as I can already visualise the look for next spring and summer. I could do it with my eyes closed in fact."

"So that gives you from October to April, minus three days to have some fun."

They sat together in silence for a while. Marco looked very serious, but finally Henry couldn't keep the stern face any longer and burst out laughing.

"What's so funny, Henry."

"You. You're funny, sitting there all gloomy and despondent. Did you honestly think I was going to let you go? You're the best thing that's ever happened in my life, and if you'll have me, I'll be here for keeps. I want you to come back to England with me and put that magic Marco makeover to good use creating our home."

Marco sat there unable to speak, tears running down his face. Henry explained that as long as he had a laptop he could work from anywhere in the world, so he suggested they live in England for the winter and then return to Holkamos for the summer season when Marco could work in the shop.

"Marco, you won't need to work. I earn enough to keep both of us, but I think that shop needs you and you also like a stage to perform on. If you weren't there, the women of Holkamos would be walking around in outfits which don't match and that would be devastating for the island."

"But I can't get over the fact that you want me. I'm loud, camp and a nobody. You could do so much better for yourself. You're educated and I can hardly write my own name, so why would you want me?"

"Because you're kind and caring, and most of all, I'm in love with you and want to spend the rest of my life with you, that's why."

Once the shock was over Marco started to get excited. He was in such a hurry to get back to the hotel, but Henry suggested they went somewhere for a drink or a coffee.

"I've not got time. I need to get to work. There's so much to sort out, and to be honest, I really don't know where to start."

"Marco, what on earth are you on about."

"The apartment, of course. How exciting it all is. I need to get my iPad and look at photos of the hall to decide on a look for it. Research the furniture and fabrics. Oh, Henry, there's so much to do."

"Before you get excited about all of that, the iPad won't be switched on tonight as I've got other plans for you."

As they walked back through the little streets of Corfu town Marco didn't stop for a breath. He went from white walls and a minimal look to rich reds and tapestries. Henry just smiled and let him continue. This was the Marco he loved, the excitable over the top bundle of fun, but the minute they got to the hotel talking about the apartment would be off limits. Henry had more important things on his mind. Come to that, so did Marco.

Chapter 34

Holkamos was starting to close down for the winter. Holidaymakers were becoming a little thin on the ground and some restaurateurs were already shutting down the restaurants and bars. The sun was still shining. It was September and people were still enjoying themselves. Nico knew he hadn't been pulling his weight and as there were no young girls to chat up he felt guilty. He let Pete and Cleo leave early, which they'd taken advantage of to go to the local restaurants which cooked the best pizzas on the island and had music and fun most nights.

"Come on, it's late. I'll walk you back down to Volmos. We can walk the pizza off."

"No, you don't have to. It's quite safe. There's always lots of visitors along that path."

"No, I want to, Cleo. We've had a lovely evening and I'd like to see the view from the castle. It's one of the things I'll miss about the island, but do you know what I'll miss the most?"

"Nico, I expect."

"I said, 'miss' not what I hope to miss. To be honest, if I never see him again, it will be too soon. No, actually that's not quite fair. If it wasn't for him, we wouldn't have had so many laughs. No, the thing I'll miss the most is you, Cleo. At the start of my stint here, all I could think about was going to Australia, but as the weeks have passed, all I can think about is you. Every morning I can't wait to go to work, to see you and be with you."

They walked up to the castle in silence. Looking down to the harbour the twinkly lights were getting switched off one by one. What was it with this view? Everyone mentioned it, but why was it so important to people? As they sat on the wall, Pete took out a bottle of wine and two glasses from his rucksack.

"What are you doing?"

"I thought it would be nice to sit here and have a drink together as we've only got a few more days left."

"What a lovely thing to do. Thank you."

They sat there looking at the little boats bobbing about in the sea, and people walking by on their way back to Volmos. It had been a very special summer for both of them. Cleo had Sarah to thank for that, and strangely enough if it hadn't been for Nico's stupid idea to have a bar, they wouldn't have even met.

"Come on. It's getting cold. Let's walk down."

Pete put his arm around Cleo's shoulders. They were both slightly giggly, but not drunk. Part way down the hill they stopped to look at Volmos, where a few yachts were moored out in the bay. Cleo turned towards Pete and looked into his eyes. They kissed for what seemed like ages, walked a bit further and then the kissing started again."

"We've wasted the whole summer. This should have happened on day one."

"No, Cleo. This is special as we've got to know each other. It's been like an old-fashioned courtship."

"You're right, Pete. It has been special."

They turned the corner and there was the house, all in darkness. Sarah had gone to bed and Henry was in Corfu with Marco.

"Would you like to come in? I hope you don't think I'm being too forward, but I think we've got some time to catch up on. I don't want to waste these last few days. Tomorrow I'm going to phone Nico and tell him we won't be in."

That's exactly what Cleo did. She also sent a text to Andréas, telling him the same thing. Andréas was quite pleased as it was the day that his mum was picking Giorgio up from the ferry. When Nico arrived, he wasn't happy. He kept wondering how strange it was that they were both ill on the same day.

"So, Nico, they're both sick?"

"Well, they didn't say they were sick. They just said they wouldn't be in, so they must be ill. What else could it be?"

Sarah was up early and as she could hear voices in Cleo's room, she knew it must be Pete as that's all her daughter had talked about for weeks. Sarah was happy about it as Pete was a nice lad. He and Cleo were both so similar, so perhaps this is what she needed, a good, sensible boyfriend. About two hours later, she heard them emerge.

"Morning, Mum. I've got something to tell you. Pete stayed last night."

"That's not a problem, but won't you both be late for work?"

"No, we're not going in today. Nico can't sack us as we finish in a few days."

"Right then, darling, I'm off to see Miriam. The house is all yours. I'll see you later."

Up in Creakos, Carolina got herself ready. She had checked the restaurant paperwork over and over again. Neither the butcher not the fishermen had been paid. The receipts from the cash and carry were in order, so she decided to break the takings down into two – the restaurant and the bar separately. She did wonder why she was bothering because as soon as Giorgio looked at it, he would blame Andréas. He would know in his heart that it was Nico, his own son, who had messed everything up rather than his nephew, but God, he would never admit that.

"Good morning, why didn't you wake me? What's the time?"

"It's nearly lunch time and it's our day off. Yes, no work for us today. Mum's gone out, so what would you like to do?"

"Go back to bed with you, if that's alright."

"Come on, give your sister a hug. "Oh, I've missed you and Holkamos has missed you too. There hasn't been a day go by when someone hasn't asked Andréas how you are. Let me take your case, the car's over there."

They drove back towards the town and then took the turning up the hill to Creakos. On the way they chatted about the hospital, his treatment and how much better he felt. The dreaded subject wasn't mentioned. Giorgio asked about his friends, Carolina's grandchildren, and all the general things that someone would ask if they had been away. When they got back to the house, Katia and the children were going to stay with her mother for the night, just to keep out of the way. All the books and restaurant paperwork were on the dining table. Giorgio had spotted them and Carolina knew that the ball was in his court. She wasn't going to say a word about them. They sat in the garden drinking coffee and enjoying the afternoon sunshine.

"Carolina, do you mind if I go and have a lie down? All this travelling has worn me out."

"Of course you can. I'm going to pop down to Miriam's for a few hours and then I'll cook us some nice swordfish. If you need anything, just phone me. I'll be a couple of hours."

Carolina knew that Giorgio might have a nap but also that he wouldn't be able to keep his hands off the restaurant books.

"Pete, we can't stay in bed all day."

"Why not? You're enjoying yourself, aren't you? I am."

"Of course. It's great, but..."

"No buts. Come here, I don't think we've practised enough, do you?"

*

The three women sat in the shade. Melvin was deadheading the cosmos which had almost become a full-time job. They chatted about everything and anything and they all enjoyed being together. Being part of this new family of people was making Sarah feel that the island was now her new home, but she had another family and other responsibilities. Also, within a short time, Miriam and Melvin would want the keys back to lock the house up for the winter and she would then be homeless.

Carolina was right. After a short nap, Giorgio got up, poured himself a glass of wine and opened the restaurant books. The takings were bad and he couldn't understand why. He looked more closely. What were all these receipts for furniture, bar equipment and cocktail glasses? Who, on Holkamos, drank cocktails? What was this other book? Why had Carolina left the takings book for another restaurant? The penny slowly dropped. Nico! What the hell was going on? No wonder Carolina had gone out without saying a word.

Back from their few days in Corfu, Marco couldn't wait to get back to the shop. He was so excited and wanted to tell Heather and Edelina his news. They were so pleased for him and the shop as he would be back for the next holiday season. They gave him an incentive, the more clothes he could sell before they closed for the winter, the more money he would have to buy next year's stock with. Marco was beginning to get a little overwhelmed with everything. He needed to go out for some fresh air. As he walked to the top of the hill and stood looking down into the harbour, he reflected on his life. I really can't believe everything that's happened, he thought. My employers trust me with their business. Not just working in it but spending thousands of their hard-earnt money. Someone loves me for being me. I'm the boy whose family disowned him, the boy that everyone teased. I'm so pleased I didn't change. I believed in myself. There were difficult times along the way, but I've come out of it as a winner.

When they finally got up, Cleo and Pete started to feel a little bit guilty. It was nearly seven o'clock. Perhaps they should go into work. Not for Nico's sake, but for Andréas and Angelo.

"Come on, Pete. Let's get the sea taxi. It's getting dark and we can see the harbour at its best."

Carolina had a few too many glasses of wine with Miriam so she decided to leave her car and walk back up to Creakos. By the time she got back to the house, Giorgio had gone over the books with a fine-toothed comb. Carolina said to herself that she wouldn't argue with him. In his heart he knew the truth, and if he wanted to blame everyone, so be it.

"Hi. How was Miriam? Did you have a nice time? I thought we could sit and have a little chat about the restaurant."

He picked up a bottle of wine and two glasses and headed out into the garden.

"Oh, Carolina, what the hell has he done? Please explain it all to me. Be honest, don't leave anything out."

Carolina told him the full story about splitting the restaurant into two and how Nico had employed Pete and Cleo who had worked their socks off for him while all he did was spend time chatting up girls. Carolina knew the bit that would upset Giorgio the most was making Angelo vacate the little flat above the restaurant.

"All these years Angelo has given his all for the business. I'm afraid Nico really has overstepped the mark this time. As far as the restaurant is concerned, as long as the bills have been paid and the staff have had their wages, I'm not too worried about it not making a lot of profit. Carolina, thank goodness it's nearly the end of the season. We can put all this behind us. I do need to consider my next move though, and I'm so sorry for all the worry you've had over these weeks."

"It's no problem, Giorgio. It's all behind us now. It's time to move forward and look to next year to get things back to normal."

"But really it's all my fault. Since his mother died I've spoilt him. I've given him whatever he wanted and made excuse after excuse for him. Every time someone criticised him, I defended him, but I know that has to stop. I need to apologise to family and friends and I need to make it up to so many people."

Andréas was the first to notice Cleo and Pete walking towards the restaurant. He had been saying for a while that it was just a matter of weeks until they got together and he was very happy for them. What were they doing here though as they had said they weren't coming in? With that they just walked in and started working without mentioning anything. Nico didn't even ask, but he did seem relieved. It was just like a normal evening although the looks between Cleo and Pete were very different. As they walked past each other, they couldn't resist a few touches. It was all very sweet.

Chapter 35

It was a new day and Giorgio had given things a lot of thought. He had talked to Andréas before he left for work and found out a few more things, but wasn't ready to go back down to Holkamos yet. He wanted to speak to Nico first and it was only fair that he gave him the opportunity to defend his actions. He decided to phone him later. In the meantime, Giorgio wanted to think things through properly. What did the future hold for him, his business and his family?

Carolina had walked back to Miriam's to collect her car and as she got there, she saw Sarah coming out.

"Hi, Carolina. Weren't we naughty yesterday drinking so much? I'm off for a walk to clear my head. Would you like to come too?"

"Sorry, but I'm in a bit of a hurry. I've only popped down to collect my car."

"Good morning, ladies. I thought I could hear talking. Have you come for the car, Carolina?"

"Yes, and I'm going for a walk to clear my head, thanks to you and all that wine, Miriam."

"Hold on, Sarah. I'll come with you if that's alright. I'll just pop in and tell Melvin. Give me a few minutes to change my shoes. Are you sure you won't join us, Carolina?"

"Oh, go on then. If you both promise there won't be any wine involved."

They walked down the lane towards the beach and instead of walking to Holkamos they turned right and walked across the sand. The sun was shining, it was a beautiful September morning and Volmos was coming alive. Holidaymakers were picking their sunbeds, the locals were arriving for an early morning swim before going off to work and out in the bay the yachts were preparing to sail around the islands.

"This is so beautiful. You're both so fortunate to have this in your life every day of the year."

"Yes, I know and even though I've lived on the island all my life, I never take it for granted. I'm so blessed."

"The silly thing is that I never wanted to come back, and if I hadn't needed to sort things out in my head, I wouldn't have. Now look at me, my daughter lives here and she's happier than ever. I've put the past right and once I came to terms with things, everything was different."

"What's that over there? I've never walked this far?"

"Oh, that's the church."

"It looks so small, and it's on the beach. How strange is that."

"Sarah, it's no ordinary church. To me, it's a very special place. It's there that I came to ask for forgiveness. It's where I confessed everything to Rex. It's special."

"My experience is very similar. When my husband, Andréas' father cheated on me very briefly, I came here for strength every day. I have a lot to thank that little building for. Yes, that church put everything right."

"Come on. Let's head back and I'll make us all a drink. I think it will be coffee today, ladies."

Andréas was setting up the restaurant. He knew today would be different, but he didn't know how things would turn out. Once Giorgio had his talk to Nico, would he be packing his bags and going or would he pull his socks up and knuckle down to work? Cleo and Pete were acting like two love birds and as usual there was no sign of Nico. That was the way they liked it. Giorgio had asked him to do one thing, text him the results and he had done so.

*

"Hi, Carolina. I need you to do something for me. Could you phone my son and ask him to pop up to your house at three o'clock on the dot? I don't want him to know it's me or else it will give him time to prepare himself. I'm sorry to ask you to do this, but I need to get things sorted. Thanks."

Carolina did as she was told and it was a long while before Nico answered. Carolina emphasised the time which he repeated, but she was putting money on it that it would be more like five o'clock than three when he eventually arrived.

Marco was going through all the clothes in the shop. He wasn't concerned that the white items weren't selling because they didn't ever go out of fashion. Lemon and pale blue were this year's colours and he needed to focus on those. September was a good month for pashminas as with the cooler evenings they practically walked out the door. Marco just needed a few ladies who were looking for several outfits to mix and match. He could do this, he knew he could.

Henry had left Marco in the shop and gone back down to Sarah's who had just returned from the walk with Miriam and was preparing herself a salad. She was so pleased to see him and to hear his plans for the hall.

"I didn't realise it was possible to be so happy, Mum. On paper we're so different, but it works well. We have so much fun together and I feel so lucky."

"Darling, when you're back in England, how are you going to explain about Marco to everyone? People can be very cruel."

"Oh, that's easy. He's my boyfriend and partner and hopefully one day my husband. If anyone's unhappy with that, I don't want them in my life. Mum, I can't thank you enough for coming to Holkamos. It's a very special island and there's something very magical, if not spiritual, about it."

"Yes, Henry, it is. Miriam and Carolina have said exactly the same and ever since I've got here I've seen how special it is too. Perhaps you're right. The island has a power that comes over you and makes you see things differently."

Henry explained that he had at least ten hours before going to meet Marco from work. He had so much to catch up on with reports that ought to have been finalised days ago, that did she mind if he just went and got on with them. Sarah was more than happy to sit in the garden reading, contemplating and planning her new life.

It was three-thirty and Nico was in no hurry to go to his aunt's. Why should he rush? All she was going to do was tell him how hard Andréas was working and all the hours he had put in. She could wait. Carolina had returned from Volmos and told Giorgio that the minute Nico pulled up in the car outside, she would go out and leave them together. Giorgio was starting to feel on edge. As the clock hands moved round, the angrier he became. Four-thirty. Then there was the sound of a car door slamming outside. Carolina nipped out of the side door and Giorgio looked at the time. Ten to five.

"Hi, Carolina, I'm here. Sorry I'm late. I had things to sort out."

Nico walked through the passage into the kitchen and as he couldn't see Carolina he walked back to the little living room. Opening the door, there was Giorgio sitting in his chair.

"Hello, Nico. I suggest you come in, sit down and start at the beginning even though you should have been here at three o'clock."

After the shock of seeing his father, Nico pulled himself together and told Giorgio the full story of how he wanted to be the first restaurant owner to bring young party visitors to Holkamos.

"Firstly, did it ever occur to you that the local residents and business owners like the town just the way it is? Perhaps they don't want a lot of party people here. It's very special here and something that we're very proud of is that the island isn't over commercialised. That's the reason why people come back year after year. Now talk to me about the wage bill."

"What do you mean, the wage bill?"

"As you can see, I've gone over the books and there appears to be two new names on the payroll. It seems they're working from ten in the morning right the way through to midnight. Can you tell me why?"

"I needed staff to make cocktails and serve them."

"So, they ran the bar and you ran the restaurant? Is that right?"

"No, Andréas ran the restaurant and I oversaw both that and the bar."

"Now you know as well as I do that not one family member or employee will tell me what you've been doing, but the other business owners will be chomping at the bit to tell me everything. Are you sure you've told me everything? You've not left anything out?"

"Alright, I've made a mistake. I shouldn't have changed things and perhaps I could have got there earlier in the mornings and stayed later at night, but I deserved to have some fun too."

"Fun, my son, happens between October and April when there are no holidaymakers, just like it has done for hundreds of years."

Giorgio had held his temper quite well so far, but he was annoyed that Nico hadn't offered any form of apology or means of putting it right. He didn't seem to have a care or thought for anyone else and didn't even ask his father how he could make it up to him.

"Can I ask why you've sneaked back without telling me you were coming? It's as if you don't trust me. All I was trying to do was make money for you, attempting to take that sad old business and stupid staff into another century."

"Shut up now, before I knock your head off those lazy shoulders. If you're so clever, how are you going to put things right?"

"Okay, so I might not have given it enough thought, but it's too late now as the season's over. Next year we'll talk about how we can do things differently."

"Right. Is that everything? I've kept quiet and calm up to now, Nico, but I've also learnt about something that's unacceptable. You had better have a very good reason for doing it because I'm telling you now, I really will knock that head off. I really will. Just one word, Angelo."

"Oh, Dad, you should have got rid of him years ago. I'm going to do up the flat over the winter and then move into it myself."

"Get out now, Nico. Go! Don't say one more word or I will."

Chapter 36

Over the next couple of days Nico kept himself busy in the restaurant. The last thing on his mind was girls as he needed to win his dad over. Andréas and the rest of the staff should have been glad that he had got his comeuppance, but strangely they felt sorry for him. Also in Creakos, Carolina was concerned about her brother and her nephew. Although she didn't have much time for Nico, as Giorgio had explained, he had spoilt him. Giorgio still hadn't calmed down and had no intention of going to the restaurant, so the only option was for Carolina to go and speak to her nephew.

Cleo wasn't as concerned about Nico as everyone else was. Why should she be? He had lied to her and used her, and she had other things on her mind. In a few days' time, Pete would be off on his big adventure to Australia, and she would be heading home to England either with or without her mother. That was another thing on her mind. She was now the product of a broken marriage.

"Hi, Nico. Have you got time for a chat?"

"Has Dad sent you down here? I've messed up. I know that, but what can I do?"

"No, your father hasn't sent me down, and yes, you have caused a lot of trouble. The business hasn't taken the money it should have done and you've spent a fortune on the bar that wasn't even necessary. You've failed to pull your weight and so it's not just your dad you should be apologising to, but all the staff who have worked so hard and kept their mouths shut for you. I know your dad will forgive you for all these things, except for throwing Angelo out. Do you know how hard he's worked for the family over the years without receiving anything other than food? There were times when there wasn't enough money to pay the wages. The other staff all left, but Angelo stood by this family because we treated him with love, kindness and respect. When your mother was so ill and your father was unable to work because of his grief, Angelo saved this business from going under. He worked night and day to keep it afloat. That's why your father is so angry."

Nico began to cry, and as much as Carolina felt sorry for him, he was a grown man who needed to take responsibility for his mistakes. All he'd wanted to do was party the summer away without thought for anyone else. Carolina had a plan to make things work without either Nico and Giorgio losing face. She explained her ideas and he had two days to get it sorted.

"Nico, before you do anything else, get rid of those bloody screens and talk to the staff. Get them on your side. Leave your father to me. This is your last chance. Do you understand?"

Over on Volmos, Miriam and Melvin were busy making plans for the winter. They were going back to England and splitting their time between Amy and Stephen's families. Sarah had asked whether the holiday let would be available for next year and this was something they needed to finalise over the winter. Heather and Edelina were going to Germany for a few weeks before returning back to commence jewellery making for their full order book. Next summer there would be more collections for more of the Greek islands. Their plans were all very exciting, and of course the best news was that Marco would be back.

Sarah was the only one who wasn't organised. Even though she did have somewhere to go in a couple of days, nothing was planned beyond that. Perhaps this was the right time to go and sort things out back at the hall, but the thought of talking to people who saw her as a victim wasn't a happy one. However, she couldn't put things off for ever and she needed to clear her head. Time to take a walk, she thought.

As she walked down the lane she bumped into Angelo who had a few hours off before his evening shift. She asked him whether he'd like to have a drink and a chat and Angelo had agreed, and so they strolled into the gardens of a hotel and found the bar. There was a lovely breeze coming from the sea. Sarah explained how everyone had been shocked and upset about the way he had been treated by Nico and that by next summer things would be back to normal. Angelo didn't see it as a problem. He was enjoying being on Volmos and in a way Nico had done him a favour. Perhaps this had been just the right thing. Sarah felt so comfortable in Angelo's company. He wasn't like the others, asking her plans, and they spent a lovely couple of hours together. Sarah was just enjoying the moment. It was nice to live just for that moment, not the past, or the future.

"Thank you, Angelo. I've had a lovely afternoon. I'm so glad I bumped into you."

"Yes, so am I. We'll see you at the restaurant before it closes for the winter."

"Yes, I couldn't leave without having one last meal there. Thank you again for today."

Sarah moved towards him and placed a kiss on his cheek. Angelo felt himself blush, but it made him feel good.

She strolled back down to the beach. She was going to miss the yachts moored in the bay and the sea taxi going back to Holkamos harbour. It had been a special summer, one that had started with her being in hiding. How ridiculous all that seemed now. No one was interested in her life. Sarah walked down to the warm water's edge, the sand felt so good on her feet. This is just me, she thought. I could tick along here to my heart's content. She carried on walking towards the jetty where more boats were moored and in the distance could see people sitting on the boats enjoying the late afternoon sunshine. There were fewer sun loungers now than in the height of summer and not many children around. She continued walking across the little bridge and there in front of her was the little church. Sarah stopped and looked at it. How could that be a church? It was only the size of a bathroom. As she took a few steps towards it, she could see a litter of wild kittens playing with some leaves, and despite preferring dogs, she knew she would miss the cats and the kittens.

As she approached the doorway and entered the church, the temperature changed. It became cooler. There were several candles burning and the pictures on the walls seemed to be staring at her. Sarah felt that they were asking her why she was there. She took a few deep breaths, held onto the back of a chair and closed her eyes. The solitude hit her, an overwhelming silence. She felt her legs turn to jelly and she began to cry real tears which rolled down her face. The silence was beginning to affect her, and she started talking out loud.

"What? Stop looking at me. I'm not the one who was in the wrong. He was the one who cheated, not me. All I did was work and make sure things ran smoothly and were organised. It was more like a business. That's what went wrong with the marriage. It was more like a business and I was a partner rather than the wife."

In her mind she could hear Miriam's voice telling her that there was no rule book and that she had to do what was best for herself. She waited until she had got her breath back and calmed down. She didn't know how long that was but finally standing up and holding onto the back of the chair, she smiled to herself. In situations such as this she would tell herself to pull herself together, but this time was different. Why should she? As she turned and walked out through the door, the heat hit her again. All she could think was thank goodness she had been in the church. If she hadn't, what was to happen next in her life would have been so different. Oh, so different.

Chapter 37

Over the last couple of days Carolina could tell Giorgio was getting bored. He was up early chatting to Andréas about the restaurant and in the evenings he couldn't wait to get back to see how things were going. He was also looking a lot better. Carolina had spoken to Nico and he was preparing to carry out her plans. Now all she had to do was persuade her brother, but there was still plenty of time for that.

In just two more days Edelina would be closing the shop. The last flights out of Preveza were in less than a week and both she and Heather were more than happy with the season's takings. It had been a lovely summer. They had never laughed so much, and most of that happiness was down to Marco. They were, however, very much looking forward to their break.

Since visiting the little church, Sarah had been busy with emails. She needed to inform the charities of her short and longer term plans. She knew they wouldn't be happy about it, but there was no going back on her decision. Cleo and Henry were sad. Cleo was saying goodbye to Pete for four or five months and who knows what could happen in that time? Although Marco would be travelling back to England, Henry knew that it wouldn't be the same as being on Holkamos. He would have to catch up with his work commitments and there would be no sunshine or sitting out in the garden with a glass or wine. Life would be very different for both of them and he felt quite sad about that. Also, neither Cleo or Henry knew about their mother's plans for the future.

*

Carolina knew she had to break the news to Giorgio. Well, part of the news. If he knew the full story, he would not be in agreement. He was sitting in the garden and so Carolina made them both a coffee and went out to talk to him.

"Oh, Giorgio, you can't stay up here forever. Your friends need to know you're back and more importantly that you're well again. Every day they come to the restaurant and ask after you. You've grown up with so many of them and even went to school with some. The season's nearly over now and some of them will be going to the mainland for the winter. You know, as well as I do, that they've all been critical about Nico and his ideas, but..."

"I know, Carolina, and I will go and see them. We're family, and as much as I'm angry with Nico, I can't let everyone see that. We've lived here all our lives, and once next season comes and the visitors start arriving again, that stupid cocktail bar will all be forgotten. Time to move on and put it all behind us."

"Oh, I'm so pleased you see it like that. Nico's not a bad lad really."

"It's my fault for spoiling him, but Carolina, I'll tell you this. The Bank of Dad has closed for one year. I need to recuperate my losses from this year. Next year is a clean slate, a fresh start, and there'll be a lot of changes."

Carolina explained her plan. No one knew Giorgio was back and so they would pretend that she had just collected him from the ferry and brought him back. They would walk into the restaurant with their heads held high. Giorgio agreed to this. As much as he realised it wasn't going to be easy, it was the best plan. He thought it odd that it should be the last ferry of the day rather than a morning one, but Carolina had planned it and he wasn't going to argue with her. After he had agreed, Carolina phoned Nico to tell him to put the plan into action and made an excuse to go out. She needed to make a lot of phone calls.

Down in the harbour, Andréas talked to all Giorgio's friends and other restaurant owners. Nico had managed to get the place looking just as it had before his father had gone into hospital and there was a real buzz to the place. Phone calls over with, it was just a question of Carolina keeping Giorgio calm and not letting him change his mind. This was a special night, not just for the family, but also for the customers who had supported the restaurant over the summer.

Miriam and Melvin had planned to have a drink with Sarah before they headed into Holkamos and Heather, Edelina, Marco and Henry were also going. Cleo and Pete were hoping to pop back for half an hour and Melvin had found a couple of bottles of champagne which had been chilling all day.

"Come on in. Oh, thank you. It should be me providing the bottles."

With that, the others arrived. Sarah had prepared some nibbles and as they didn't need to be in Holkamos for a couple of hours, they were all laughing and joking. Marco was showing them photos of the hall that he had downloaded onto his phone.

"Now, Marco. You're right, that's the hall, and if you look very carefully, those two windows in the top left hand corner are the rooms where we'll be living."

Miriam wanted to know his ideas for interior design. Marco was so excited about everything, that he even had photos of clothes he thought were suitable to wear in a castle.

"No, Marco. It's not a castle. It's just a hall."

In walked Cleo and Pete. Nico had told them there was no need to hurry back as the restaurant was only open to invited guests and he could manage as it was going to be a buffet.

"Well, this is it, Mum, our last night on Volmos. Where has the summer gone? It seems to have flown by?"

"I know, Cleo. I think I should say a few words. Firstly, a huge thank you to Miriam and Melvin for letting me stay here and making me feel so welcome. Also, of course, a huge thank you to Marco for giving me one of his now very famous makeovers. It's been one of my highlights. Then, Cleo and Henry for being able to spend precious time with you both and for the beautiful memories we've created. It's been so very special, but my biggest thanks goes to Holkamos and down here on Volmos. I felt as though the island wrapped its arms around me when I arrived and whispered that I'm safe. It will look after me. That's just exactly what the island has done. It's given me time and breathing space, but most of all it's shown me love. Soon it's going to leave me with an image that sums up this beautiful island – the breathtaking view from the sea taxi as we arrive in the harbour."

There were hugs and kisses and a toast to the island before they all made their way down to the jetty to catch the taxi. As they stood waiting, Sarah looked towards the little church in the distance, touched her mouth and blew a kiss. Thank you, Volmos.

At the restaurant the locals had gathered together with gifts waiting for Giorgio to arrive.

"Come on. It's time to go. Are you sure you're up for this? It's not too late to change your mind."

"Oh, Carolina. What would you do if I said I wasn't going? Come on, let's get it over with, but before you go, I want to pass something by you. If you think it's a bad idea, just say so. I won't be offended, but the thing is I've been thinking about my future. I'm not getting any younger and also my health isn't brilliant, so I..."

Sarah and the others were the only passengers on the little boat and she could feel the butterflies in her stomach. Not because it was her last time on the boat, but because it always made her feel like this. As the boat went around the cliff, there it was, twinkling, shining and looking so stunning. Holkamos harbour never failed to impress her. Just like Sarah, everyone felt the same. It wasn't just the view. It was much than that, so much more.

The restaurant was full of customers who had become friends over the years. Carolina stopped the car in a back road, forgetting that they would have to walk past Giorgio's house, the house that had been in the family for hundreds of years. He stopped and stared and Carolina could see the tears in his eyes. He took some deep breaths. Carolina understood that lots of people over the years had said that's the first thing they do when they come back to the island – breathe in the beautiful, clean air and smell the scent of the island. It was like nowhere else they'd ever been. As they got nearer the restaurant, Giorgio wasn't surprised to see so many people there. It was part and parcel of what always happened when someone returned. They are always welcomed back with open arms.

For the next two hours Giorgio chatted and made small talk with everyone. He thanked people for their kindness and told them how much he'd missed the island and his family. He even had a laugh with Pete and Cleo for quite a while. Nico noticed this and wondered what they were talking about. He didn't understand the ritual of welcoming someone back, but people loved this place as though it was sacred and it all seemed rather strange to him.

"Before you all start to leave, I'd just like to say a few

words. Thank you all so much for coming. It's lovely to be back and I've missed you and the island so much. A huge thank you to Nico for giving up his very busy life to come back and run the business while I've been in hospital."

Everyone looked at each other, but they understood. What else he could say, although Nico was more shocked than anyone.

"I'd also like to thank all my staff for working so hard this season. I know it's not been the most straightforward one, and especially my very special sister who yet again has held the family and business together. I don't want to say any more, except for just one thing and that's I'm going to be semi retiring from the restaurant. That's not to say I won't be around. Try stopping me. It gives me so much pleasure to say that my nephew, Andréas, has agreed to take over the business as from next year. He's worked here all his life and shares the same love and passion for it as I do and my father and grandfather before me. I'm sure you'll all wish Andréas health and happiness with his future plans as over the winter we plan to continue the refurbishment that Nico has started and that includes Angelo's little flat as I've promised him some air conditioning. So if he disappears in the summer you'll know where to find him, his little home above the restaurant. And one more thing, both Pete and Cleo have agreed to come back and work with Andréas and the team next year when they're back from their adventure."

"No, it's only Pete who's going to Australia. I'm not."

"Why not, Cleo. Don't you want to spend time with me?"

"Of course, I do, but it's your adventure, not mine."

"No, my darling. It's ours, that's if you want it."

"Yes, more than anything else in the world."

"So, that's all sorted then. Oh, there is just one more

thing. I'm moving up to live with Carolina in Creakos and Andréas, Katia and the children are moving into the family home down here in the harbour. Thank you all again. I've missed you and this is a very special island."

"Father, why haven't you discussed any of this with me? What am I going to do?"

"Nico, when have you ever told me what you're up to? You were born and grew up on Holkamos, but you don't have the same love for it. Go off, enjoy the world and have fun. The world is your oyster, as they say."

Carolina went over to Andréas, held him tightly and whispered in his ear how very proud she was of him. It was so exciting. The business was being passed down to the next generation.

Sitting on the sea wall, looking out to the horizon, Sarah was in a little world of her own. A world that she had to leave behind. It was time to move on, time for a fresh start.

"A penny for your thoughts, Sarah."

"Miriam, they're free to you. Thank you again for everything you've done for me."

You don't need to keep thanking me, Sarah. You paid your rent and kept the house perfect."

"No, not just for the house, but for the advice which I've listened to over and over again in my head. I don't care what people think. I've thrown the rule book away and I'm doing what my heart tells me to do."

"And what would that be?"

"It's telling me to give us a second chance. Not him, but us. I was as much to blame as him as I was far too ambitious. If I had given him more of me and my time, perhaps he wouldn't have made all the mistakes he did."

"We all make mistakes. Some get found out, others stay a secret, but what matters is what you do with the secret."

THE END

Also by Ian Wilfred

Putting Right The Past
The Little Terrace of Friendships
A Secret Visitor to Saltmarsh Quay
Secrets We Left in Greece

Printed in Great Britain
by Amazon